IMAGES
of America

FORT ATKINSON

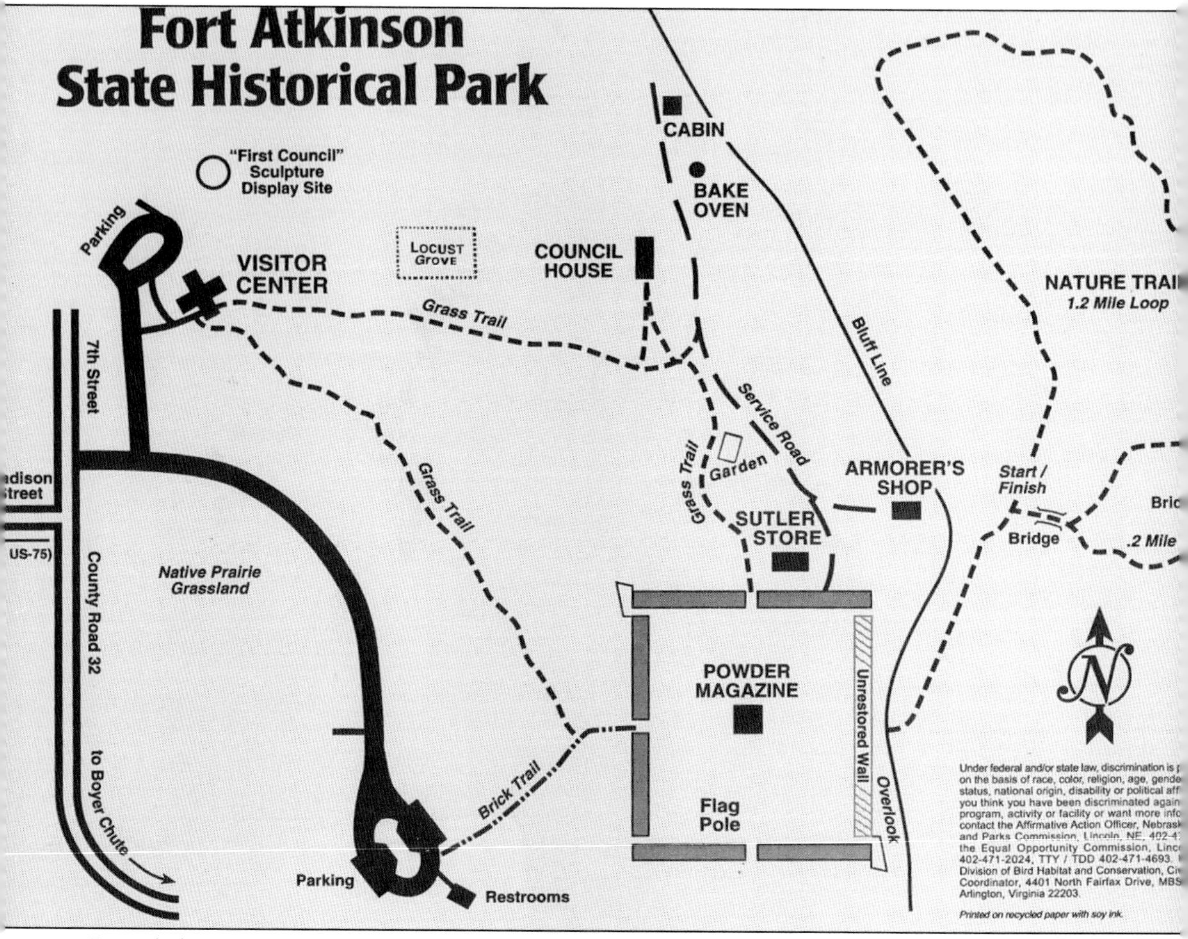

Provided to guests at the historical park's visitor center, this map of present-day Fort Atkinson's layout shows the location of features of the original fort that have been reconstructed to date plus modern-day features. Those visiting the park can do so for the price of a Nebraska State Parks day pass per carload of people, even on living history weekends.

On the Cover: Well-known Omaha photographer Louis Bostwick snapped this 1927 picture at the dedication ceremony for the flagpole monument erected by the Daughters of the American Revolution to mark the site. As the plaque indicates, it was 100 years since the abandonment of old Fort Atkinson. In the midst of an empty cornfield at the time, it is now encompassed by the restored walls of the fortress. (Washington County Museum.)

IMAGES
of America

FORT ATKINSON

Kenneth C. Flint

ARCADIA
PUBLISHING

ISBN 978-0-7385-8353-2

Published by Arcadia Publishing
Charleston, South Carolina

Printed in the United States of America

Library of Congress Control Number: 2010933170

For all general information, please contact Arcadia Publishing:
Telephone 843-853-2070
Fax 843-853-0044
E-mail sales@arcadiapublishing.com
For customer service and orders:
Toll-Free 1-888-313-2665

Visit us on the Internet at www.arcadiapublishing.com

To the memories of those many departed souls who have given Fort Atkinson its life, both the hundreds who inhabited the past fort and those who have left us during its present incarnation.

This includes SHP assistant superintendent Jerry Farber (seen on page 98) who so ably and enthusiastically served the park and living history program for many years before passing away in 2003.

Sadly, there was another loss to Fort Atkinson during the preparation of this book. Edwin "Eddie" Wood (seen on page 121), son of longtime interpreter Tom Wood and himself a volunteer 6th Infantry soldier, was killed in action on July 5, 2010, serving his country as a real U.S. Army soldier in Afghanistan—just one month before his 19th birthday.

Both men are sorely missed by the Friends of Fort Atkinson.

Contents

Acknowledgments

Special thanks go to Stephen Kemper, the first superintendent of Fort Atkinson State Historical Park (SHP); John Slader, the present superintendent; and Faith Norwood, the curator of the Washington County Museum for their assistance in compiling the information and utilizing the resources of their archives. I am also much in debt to my fellow members of the Friends of Fort Atkinson who provided information and photographs of the living history years.

Other sources of information and images for this book that must be acknowledged include the following: the Blair *Enterprise* and *Pilot-Tribune* newspapers, the Fort Atkinson Foundation, the Nebraska Game and Parks Commission, the Nebraska State Historical Society, the *Omaha World-Herald*, and the U.S. National Archives.

Where an image source is not specifically identified, it was found in the archives of Fort Atkinson SHP.

Finally, many thanks are owed to editor Ted Gerstle for accepting me as author and shepherding me through my first book for Arcadia.

Bibliography

Carlson, Gayle F. *Archeological Investigations at Fort Atkinson*. Lincoln, NE: Nebraska State Historical Society, 1979.

Kivett, Marvin F. "Excavations at Fort Atkinson Nebraska, a Preliminary Report." *Nebraska History*. Lincoln, NE: Nebraska State Historical Society, 1959.

Ney, Virgil. *Fort on the Prairie: Fort Atkinson on the Council Bluff 1819–1827*. Washington D.C.: Command Publications, 1978.

Introduction

Fort Atkinson today is a rare and remarkable site that should probably not exist. It was an amazing combination of luck, faith, money, and effort that brought about the literal resurrection of the long-vanished citadel from an empty field. Without the efforts of those 100 years ago, the location of the fort would have been forgotten. Without the investigations of archaeologists to identify the foundations, they would have been destroyed. Without the fund-raising and contributions of thousands of Nebraskans, the site would not have been purchased and preserved. Without the efforts of the Nebraska Game and Parks Commission and more generous contributions, the fort would not have been rebuilt. And without the loyalty and labor of so many volunteers, the living history program would not exist.

As the separate chapters of this book more greatly detail, the life, death, and reincarnation of this unique historical spot came in several distinct stages. In 1819, the fortification was erected on the Council Bluff high above the Missouri River's western bank. After the fort's original, brief life as the key and solitary U.S. bastion protecting a vast western frontier, it was abandoned in 1827. The structures fell quickly into ruin and soon all but vanished beneath the prairie sod.

Still, though the fort was gone, it was not forgotten. Migrating Mormons used brick salvaged from the ruins to build their summer quarters. By the 1850s, pioneers were settling the area, establishing the town site of Fort Calhoun, Nebraska. In the late 1800s, town resident W. H. Woods was investigating the remains. Other locals interested in the fort began a movement to preserve the location. Nothing concrete was accomplished, however, and it seemed that what was left of Fort Atkinson, now under a farm field, would be plowed out of existence or overbuilt by a housing development.

Then, in the late 1950s, a new hope for salvation arose. It was inspired by the archaeological digs of the Nebraska State Historical Society, which proved that cellars, foundations, other substantial features, and a wealth of artifacts remained beneath the croplands. When this galvanized the public to action, a Fort Atkinson Foundation was formed. Supported by thousands of people from across the state and the country and assisted by organizations like the *Omaha World-Herald*, it accomplished the enormous task of raising funds to buy the site. In 1963, the land was given over to the Nebraska Game and Parks Commission to be developed as a state historical park.

With the park established in 1970, plans proceeded with creating an interpretive site for tourists. This first involved rebuilding the original fort's corner bastions and gateways to define its shape and dimensions for visitors. Following this came better site access, parking, restrooms, and the first visitors center. By the late 1970s, restoration plans had gone much further. One section of the western line of the square fort's walls—each side 200 yards long—was rebuilt, and work on a second section had begun.

The 1980s saw massive construction underway, both to restore the fort and to build modern park facilities. Generous contributions allowed efforts to proceed first on the south barracks line, followed by the north line. Other separate structures of the old fort were reconstructed, including the armory, trapper's cabin, council house, and powder magazine. More importantly, a large, modern visitors center was opened containing a museum, theater, and animated displays.

A living history program, started in the 1980s, began to grow rapidly in the 1990s and was officially organized into the Friends of Fort Atkinson. Scores of volunteers interested in interpreting the fort era repopulated the restored stronghold. Scenarios demonstrating every aspect of 1820s-era life, both military and civilian, were developed. Rooms in the rebuilt barracks were fitted out to represent kitchens, quarters for officers and men, a hospital, cooper and carpenter shops, and a blacksmith among many others.

By the first decade of the new century, fort volunteers were also creating more elaborate and special scenarios for occasions like Independence Day. Additional interpretive sites were being established. Other fort structures, like a sutler's store, were built. Planning was also underway for improvements to the site and living history program and for maintaining what had already been accomplished for generations to come.

One thing has united all those who have contributed to the rebirth: a deep affection for Fort Atkinson and what it represents. Its spirit truly takes hold of those who come here. What it was nearly two centuries ago and what it could become again has seized the imagination of many.

In the late 1800s, it was W. H. Woods who told Nebraskans it was time to "help the young people to study sunshine, charity and history" by "securing means from the government to purchase old Ft. Atkinson," create a national cemetery for the hundreds buried there, and "all stand up for Nebraska and her honored dead."

A century ago, the Nebraska State Historical Society made a strong plea for the establishment of a park on that site. Such places of historic interest would "grow into objects of perpetual pilgrimage and patriotic inspiration." The Council Bluff plateau at Fort Calhoun would become another Plymouth Rock in interest and attraction, visited by tourists from all parts of the world.

In the 1920s, it was a young Fort Calhoun resident named Edith Neale, already embarked on a lifelong crusade to preserve the fort, who wrote passionately of creating a fitting memorial and helped collect money to create a first museum of fort artifacts.

Fifty years ago it was the first prospectus of a newly founded Fort Atkinson Foundation that declared the intention of "restoration of this important milepost of America's growth" to "perpetuate a glorious heritage of brave enterprise to inspire Americans of many generations hence." This, finally, initiated the successful effort to rescue and restore this rare jewel of Americana from the really old Old West.

Over the following years, many more would fall under the spell of what famed Nebraska author Marie Sandoz called the "most romantic" frontier post. All of us who love the fort and are dedicated to its preservation can, I think, identify with the sentiments expressed by the park's first superintendent, Stephen Kemper. He was the one first faced with the daunting task of raising the fallen fortress from the earth of a farm field.

"I really became immersed in the fort," he said. "The thought of the great amount of suffering and death that these individuals endured on the Council Bluff led me to feel that the reconstruction would serve as a reminder to citizens today of these soldiers' and civilians' sacrifices. Something about the place, just the feeling that is elicited as you walk over that deserted parade ground on a quiet moonlit night—I think that something just reached out and touched my soul."

Some 50 years of continuous effort by many organizations and individuals succeeded in resurrecting much of the bastion called Fort Atkinson. And 30 years of volunteer involvement brought that fortress back to life. The continued interest and support of Nebraskans, American patriots, and all those who love history will insure that this vital site will not once again sink beneath the sod but survive and grow into the far future.

One

Old Fort Atkinson

It was a mighty undertaking. As the first American expedition into the vast new western territories following Lewis and Clark, it involved one-fifth of the U.S. Army—1,126 elite men. This dauntless force was launched on a daring enterprise that might be seriously compared to America's missions to the moon—except that these men had gone to stay. In 1819, they battled hundreds of miles up the wild Missouri River from St. Louis on primitive steamboats and keels. After a four-month quest, they reached the same Council Bluff where the famous duo first met with Native American tribes. Here the already exhausted men survived a winter plagued by severe weather, near-starvation, a scurvy epidemic felling hundreds, and a devastating flood. They hung on by courage and sheer doggedness to begin building a fortress high atop the bluff.

This site "on Earth's remotest bounds," as one journalist dubbed it, became the stage for the saga of the far-frontier bastion to be called Fort Atkinson. As this country's first major settlement west of the Missouri, it was the site of many firsts for both America and what would be Nebraska, including the western territory's first library, school, newspaper, hospital, factories, and farms. The fort faced threats from Indian tribes, the British, and nature itself. Its military might protected America's interests and the burgeoning fur trade, provided a base camp for explorations, and concluded numerous treaties. Its tale is filled with the names of military heroes like Riley and Leavenworth, the friends and relatives of Lewis and Clark, famed explorers like Long and Kearney, and folklore figures like Jim Bridger, Mike Fink, and Hugh Glass.

The fort's life, however, though glorious, was very brief. By 1827, the shifting policies of western expansion dictated a different location for such a military presence. The 6th Infantry left its "Elysian Fields" to move south and build Fort Leavenworth. The great fort on the bluff was abandoned, and the wooden structures fell into ruins, so swiftly that an 1833 painting by artist Carl Bodmer showed little but the brick chimneys still erect.

Lewis and Clark were the earliest American visitors to the site. On August 3, 1804, they held the first formal meeting between U.S. representatives and the western Indian tribes. The groups met in the shade of the expedition keelboat's main sail, which was set up as an awning. This momentous parley brought them to name the commanding spot above the river "The Council Bluff." (Nebraska Game and Parks.)

It was the expansionist political philosophy of John C. Calhoun, the U.S. secretary of war under Pres. James Monroe, which created Fort Atkinson. Following the then recent (1812–1814) war against Britain, he was suspicious of alliances between the British and many American Indian tribes and devised a strategy to secure U.S. control of the new Northwest Territories.

Col. Henry Atkinson, a War of 1812 veteran, was chosen to lead what was called the Yellowstone Expedition. Its original intent was to build a string of defensive forts up the Missouri to the Yellowstone River. However, cuts in federal funding caused the expedition to be halted at its first stop, the Council Bluff.

This portion of an 1820 map based upon information from the Yellowstone Expedition shows the route of the months-long 700-mile journey upriver from St. Louis (lower right). It was made mostly by dragging or poling a fleet of keelboats. The site of the fort is labeled as Fort Calhoun (upper left). It was originally assumed that it would be called so in honor of the expedition's founder.

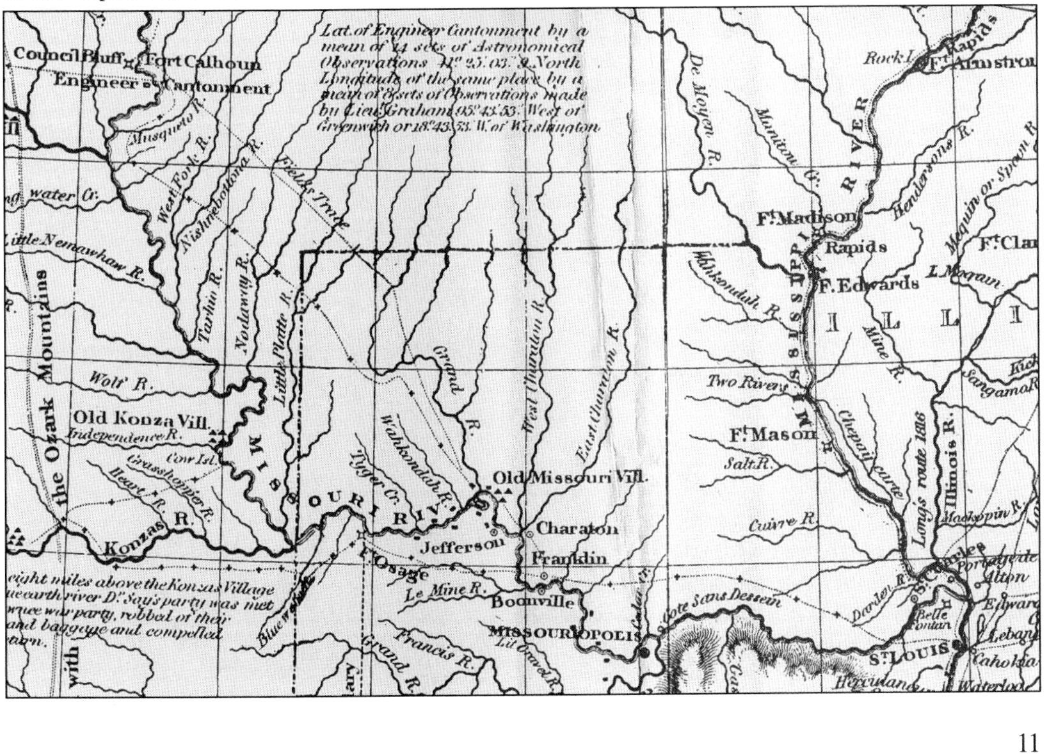

The main military contingent included in the expedition was the elite 6th Infantry Regiment. During the War of 1812, at the Battle of Chippewa, the veteran soldiers who would form the 6th advanced without wavering through a hail of enemy fire. The British commander, at first thinking them undisciplined militia, realized his mistake and cried, "Those are Regulars, by God!" This became their motto.

The 1st Regiment of Riflemen, also very active in the War of 1812, was another element of the expedition. This unique unit, with its distinctive green, gold-fringed frocks and Harpers Ferry rifles, was a part of the Fort Atkinson garrison until it was amalgamated into the 6th Infantry in 1821. Here a general and a regimental staff officer examine a map, while riflemen in summer undress form ranks behind.

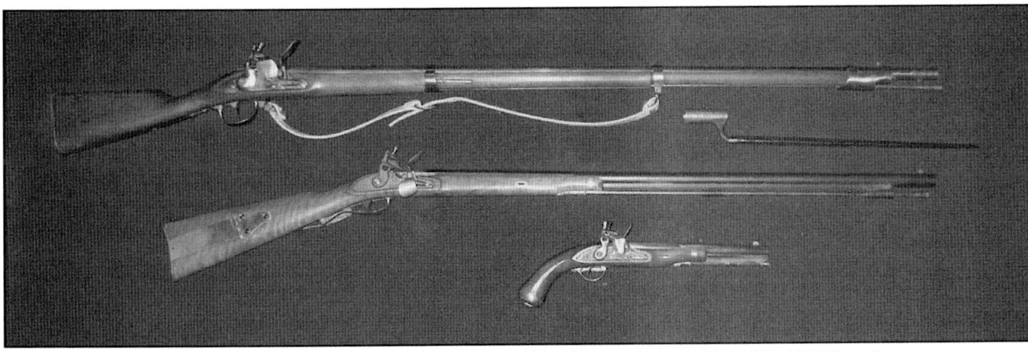

The weapons of the fort's era were flintlocks firing black powder and lead ball. The three main types of gun used by the soldiers were (from top to bottom) the Infantryman's .69-caliber smoothbore musket, the Rifleman's .54-caliber rifle, and the officer's .58-caliber pistol. Many of these were produced at the Harpers Ferry and Springfield Armories.

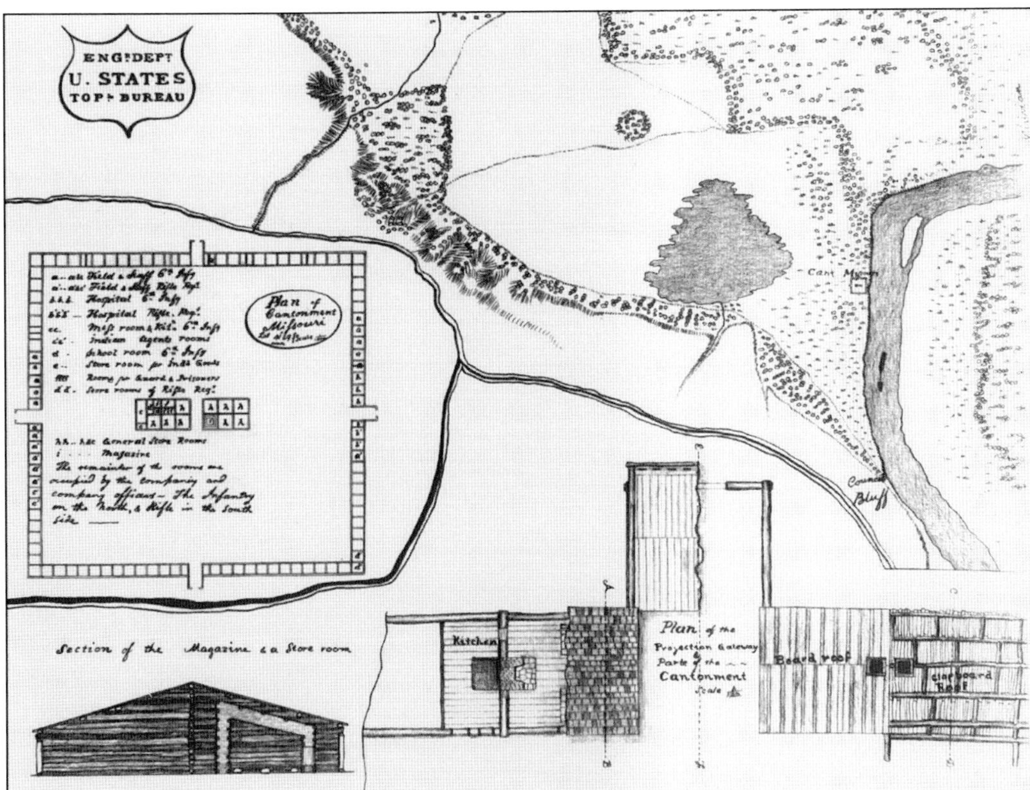

Lewis and Clark had recommended building atop the bluff, but the first fort, called Cantonment Missouri, was built on the river's edge a mile north. It was a bad idea. After the first, brutal winter, a massive spring flood washed the fort away, forcing the army to seek higher ground. This plan, drawn by expedition engineer Lt. Andrew Talcott, is all that remains of the first fort. (National Archives.)

A separate scientific expedition led by Stephen. H. Long accompanied the military one. Wintering just south of the Council Bluff in 1819, it then explored the Platte River to the mountains, returning along the border with the Spanish colonies. Long claimed that the plains area was a "Great American Desert" unsuitable for agriculture. This was something that the garrison of Fort Atkinson would disprove. (National Park Service.)

The *Missouri Intelligencer and Boonslick Advertiser* was the closest newspaper to the Council Bluff, being at Franklin, Missouri, 350 miles away. This issue carries a story on Long's expedition, giving the "history of the expedition from Pittsburg [*sic*] to the Rocky Mountains in the year 1819, under the command of Major Long."

Missouri Intelligencer.

NO. 19] FRANKLIN, MISSOURI, DECEMBER 10, 1822. [VOL. IV.

PRINTED EVERY TUESDAY,
BY
Patten & Cleveland,
Publishers of the Laws of the United States.

CONDITIONS.

Two dollars and fifty cents per annum payable in advance, or three dollars at the expiration of the year.

Those who do not, at the end of the year, direct their papers to be discontinued, will be considered as engaged for the next. None will be discontinued until all arrearages are paid, unless at the option of the editors.

The following gentlemen are authorised to receive subscriptions and moneys for the Editors:

Clay County—Wm. L. Smith, Esq.
Ray County—John T. Beach, Esq.
Chariton County—Col. James [illegible]
Cooper—Robert P. Clark, Esq.

MISCELLANEOUS.

EXPEDITION TO THE ROCKY MOUNTAINS.

FROM THE NATIONAL GAZETTE.

Extracts from the history of the expedition from Pittsburg to the Rocky Mountains, in the year 1819, under the command of Major Long.

On the [illegible] of October, four hundred Omawhaw Indians assembled at Camp Missouri.—Major O'Fallon addressed them in an appropriate speech, stating the reasons for their being called to council, upon which *Ongpa tonga*, the *Big-Elk*, arose and after shaking by hand each of the whites present, placed his robe of Otter skins and his mockasins under the feet of the agent, whom he addressed to the following effect, as his language was interpreted by Mr. Dougherty.

"He had heard that his father [illegible] have injured you so well, you surely would treat your poor children, the Omawhaws, who have never done harm to your people, with much kindness also. But I am afraid the transaction will have a bad effect on my young men. When they heard of American troops ascending this river, they feared and respected them. But I am fearful that this transaction will throw them off their guard, make them lose their respect for you, and cause them to do something that they would not otherwise have done, and thus create trouble and difference between us. You said, my father, that those troops do not come to harm us. I believe it is true.—I consider them as my brothers and friends. So far from thinking they come to [illegible] me, I regard them as my shield, to guard me against bad nations around me. You say, that if ever there is a difference between us, that it will be our fault; but I hope not, my father, I cannot think that the Omawhaws will offer any indignity to your people, now that they have seen all those troops, when they have not harmed individuals who have resided years in their villages unprotected, although we were then less enlightened than we now are. Some think, my father that you have brought all these warriors here to take our land from us, but I do not believe it. For although I am but a poor simple Indian, yet I know that this land will not suit your farmers; if I even thought your hearts bad enough to take the land, I would not fear it, as I know there is not wood enough on it for the use of the whites. You might settle along this river, where timber [illegible] born in the prairie;" and subsequently, "I told you, my father, to look at me, that you might see if there is any of the blood of your people upon me. Some, whose hands have been stained with blood, endeavor to wash it off, but some of it will still remain."

It is proper to mention, as explanatory of some of the allusions in the above speeches, that the Pawnees, at the conclusion of their council, had been invited to dine at Camp Missouri, and that many of their chiefs were there presented with sabres, as I before stated. It was to this circumstance, that the above mentioned speakers had reference, as being inexplicable to them, as it seemed as if we wished to conciliate the good will of these evil doers through fear, and yet they could hardly accuse us of fear, surrounded as we were by so formidable an array of troops.

—

In the year 1814, a trader married a beautiful squaw of one of the most distinguished families in the Omawhaw nation. This match on the part of the husband, was induced by the following circumstances. Being an active, intelligent and enterprising man, he had introduced the American trade to the Missouri Indians, and had gained great influence amongst them by his bravery and ingenuous deportment. But he, at length, perceived that his influence was gradually declining, in consequence of the presence and wiles of many rival traders, to whom his enterprize had opened the way, and that his customers were gradually forsaking him.

Thus circumstanced in order to [illegible] The agreement being thus concluded, the trader made presents agreeably to the custom of the nation, and conducted his interesting prize to his house.

The ensuing autumn she had the pleasure to see him return, having now conceived for him the most tender attachment. Upon his visit the following season, she presented him with a fine daughter, born during his absence, and whom she had nursed with the fondest attention.—With the infant in her arms, she had daily seated herself on the bank of a river, and followed the downward course of the stream, with her eye, to gain the earliest notice of his approach. Thus time passed on. The second year the father greeted a son, and obtained his squaw's reluctant consent to take their daughter with him on his return voyage to the country of the white people. But no sooner had he commenced his voyage, although she had another charge upon which to lavish her caresses, than her maternal fondness overpowered her and she ran crying and screaming along the river side in pursuit of the boat, tearing out her long flowing hair, and appearing to be almost bereft of reason. On her returning home she gave away every thing she possessed, cut off her hair, went in deep mourning, and remained inconsolable. She would often say that she well knew that her daughter would be better treated, than she could be at home, but she could not avoid regarding her own situation to be the same as if the Wahconda had taken away her offspring forever.

One day in company with six o[illegible] ly. On the succeeding day the trader sent for his squaw and after making her some presents, he directed her to accompany her friends who were then on their way to their hunting grounds.

She departed without a murmur as it is not unusual with the Omawhaws to send off one of their wives on some occasions, while they remain with the favorite one.

About two months afterwards the trader recalled her. Overjoyed with what she supposed to be her good fortune, she lost no time in presenting herself before the husband whom she tenderly loved.—But great was her disappointment when her husband demanded the surrender of the child, and announced for the future any association with herself, directing her to return to her people, and to provide for her future well-being, in any way she might choose.

Overpowered by her feelings on this demand and repudiation, she ran from the house, and finding a periouge on the river, she paddled over to the opposite side and made her escape into the forest, with her child. The night was cold and attended with a fall of snow and hail. Reflecting upon her disconsolate condition, she resolved to return again in the morning, and, with the feelings of a wife and a mother, to plead her cause before the arbiter of her fate, and endeavor to mitigate the cruel sentence.

Agreeably to this determination, she once more approached him, upon whom she had claims paramount to those of any other individual.—"Here is our child," said she, "I do not question your fondness for [illegible]

The army was supplied with three steamboats for the trip. However, only the steamboat for Long's expedition, the *Western Engineer*, survived the treacherous waters of the Missouri to reach the Council Bluff, becoming the first steamboat to ascend so far up the river. It is depicted here by expedition artist Titian Peale at the expedition's camp, called Engineer Cantonment. (American Philosophical Society, Philadelphia.)

Soon after the arrival of the Yellowstone Expedition at the Council Bluff, Benjamin O'Fallon, the expedition's Indian agent, held a major parley with over 70 of the Pawnee tribe's chiefs. This painting by Samuel Seymour, another artist with the Long Expedition, portrays the October 1819 council. It was held at the Engineer Cantonment.

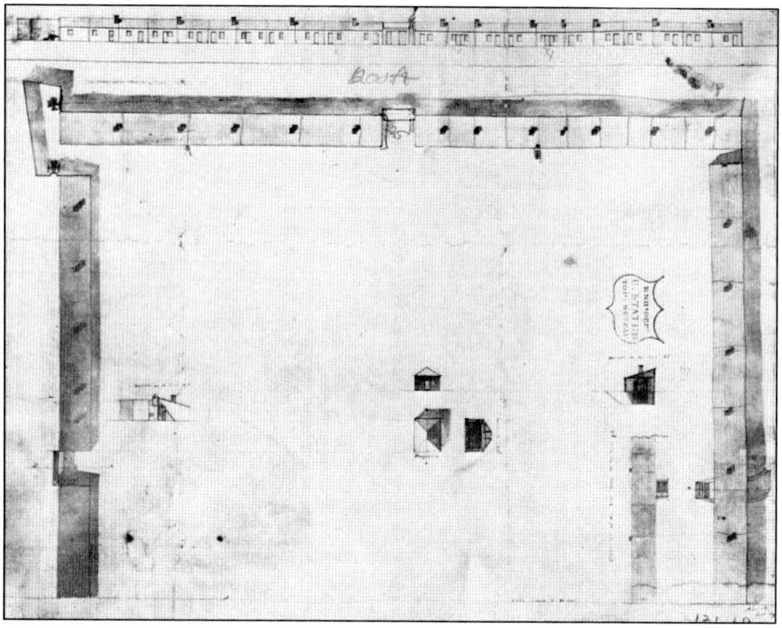

By the following winter of 1820, the troops had constructed their second fort, which was to be named Fort Atkinson. This plan of it, also by Talcott, shows the northern half of the fort, including two gates, a bastion, the powder magazine, and a passageway under the east wall. This plan proved very useful in restoring the fort accurately. (National Archives.)

This 1973 painting by Blair artist Alton Larsen depicts the fort in its heyday. Based on research and archaeological evidence, it shows the quadrangle of barracks buildings and some of the estimated 50 outbuildings. There is a brick factory to the lower left, a blacksmith shop below the bluff, and a passageway under the east wall to the right. (Washington County Museum.)

With the addition of Illinois to the United States in 1818, it was the 21-star flag that first flew over Fort Atkinson. Over the fort's lifetime, 23-star (with new states Alabama in 1819 and Maine in 1820) and 24-star (with new state Missouri in 1821) flags would also wave proudly from its flagpole. No 22-star flag was ever produced.

In 1823, a party of 70 trappers under Gen. William Ashley was attacked by a party of 600 well-armed Arikara warriors below their fortified villages (at top). The trappers were high on the Upper Missouri, in what is now North Dakota. Their party included famed frontiersmen Jed Smith, Jim Bridger, the Sublette brothers, and Hugh Glass. Twelve men were killed and many more wounded, including Glass.

Col. Henry Leavenworth replaced Atkinson as commander of the fort in 1821. After the attack on Ashley, he led companies of the 6th Infantry 700 miles up the Missouri in keelboats to attack the Arikara villages. It was the first full-scale engagement between the Plains Indians and the U.S. Army in American history. He is now most famous for the founding of Fort Leavenworth in Kansas.

Many famous explorers and fur traders of the era visited the fort. Jim Bridger (seen here in his 50s) was a member of Ashley's party at age 17. It was he and John Fitzgerald who abandoned a supposedly dying Hugh Glass after his famed run-in with a grizzly bear. Glass survived to hunt the two down. He forgave Bridger. He found Fitzgerald at Fort Atkinson, protected by having enlisted as a soldier.

In September 1824, Benjamin O'Fallon arranged for a Mexican delegation from Santa Fe to visit Council Bluff. They came to negotiate a peace treaty with the Pawnee, who had been raiding their communities. The successful outcome of this meeting was the first and, to date, only international treaty worked out in what would become Nebraska.

In 1825, now General Atkinson and Indian agent O'Fallon traveled up the Missouri with 475 soldiers to negotiate treaties with tribes along the river. Their method of transportation was unique; Atkinson decided to use experimental wheel boats on the 3,000-mile trip. As illustrated in a sketch by Neil Johnson, soldiers powered the boats by pulling and pushing crossbars connected by Pitman gears to side-mounted paddle wheels. (Washington County Museum.)

With the thrust of westward settlement shifted to the southwest and the fur trade's protection secured by treaties, a military post at the Council Bluff was no longer necessary. On the morning of June 6, 1827, the 6th Infantry formed up on its parade ground a final time. The men boarded boats and sailed away southward, catching their last glimpse ever of the walls, bastions, and flagpole of proud old Fort Atkinson.

After Fort Atkinson was abandoned by the army, its soft, cottonwood walls soon fell into disrepair. What remained was also pillaged and likely burned by the local tribes. When artist Carl Bodmer visited the site in 1833, this detail from his painting of the Council Bluff showed that little remained but the brick chimneys, thrusting up forlornly. There is a ruined brick factory to the far left. (Northern Natural Gas Collection, Joslyn Art Museum.)

Two

Keeping the Past Alive

Although the fort disappeared, its location was never lost. Just 20 years after its abandonment, Mormon pioneers migrating westward salvaged brick from the ruins to create their summer quarters. By the 1850s, settlers were establishing the town site of Fort Calhoun in what had become Washington County, Nebraska. In 1855, the first families arrived, scavenging more remnants to build their homes. Enough still remained into the next century that locals could identify the depressions of building locations and gather large amounts of artifacts. But when a farm was established on the top of the bluff, seasonal plowing began to gradually but inevitably erase the visible remains.

Over the years, there was sporadic interest in the site and its preservation. A 1919 centennial celebration of the fort's founding was the first major event to recognize its historical value. From this arose a movement of individuals interested in conserving at least some of the fort's remains. Contributions from them went toward creating a museum to display some of the many artifacts. In 1927, the Daughters of the American Revolution erected a flagpole on a brick monument base at the site. By this point there was an effort afoot to make the farm into a state park. For the first time, the notion was advanced that the fort could actually be restored.

However, none of this coalesced into a solid movement to preserve the site. It would be yet another 30 years before anything was done. By that time, little was left to mark the location of the battlements but that DAR flagpole—a lonely object in the midst of an empty plain. The decades of farming had all but erased the fort's footprint. And now a proposed housing development threatened to obliterate the site forever.

Desperate to establish the existence of the fort's remains before it was too late, the state historical society did some archaeological investigations in 1956. Though small, the dig made some significant finds. Fort Atkinson's foundations were still there, beneath the prairie sod. Their rediscovery would begin a new, more determined movement to save the remnants from destruction.

William Henry Woods (affectionately known locally as Granddaddy) was one of the first to raise interest in preserving the fort. A Civil War veteran, he moved to Fort Calhoun in the late 1800s and began to explore the fort site, collecting many artifacts. Here he examines a major find—an intact plowshare exemplifying the garrison's extensive agricultural pursuits. (Washington County Museum.)

Woods created the first museum of fort artifacts at his own home in Fort Calhoun. This 1905 photograph shows just one part of his huge collection, displayed outside his shed. Visible in the various sections are keys, locks, horseshoes, hinges, nails, buckles, pipes, gun parts, tools, and even Indian relics, a cross-section representing daily life at the fort. (Washington County Museum.)

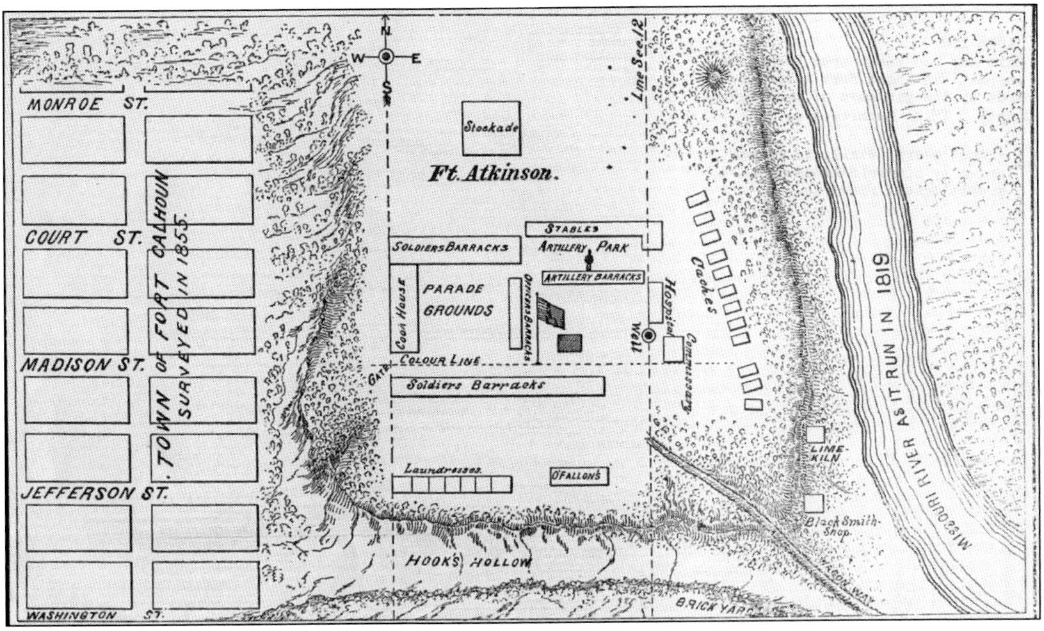

In 1892, Woods toured the site with Capt. Benjamin Contal, who was born to a drum major father and laundress mother at the fort in 1819. Because he was a small child then, his remembrances were likely more guesses than facts. As a result, a map drawn up by Martha Turner from the information was more than a bit fanciful, as can be seen by comparing it to Talcott's plan (see page 16). (Washington County Museum.)

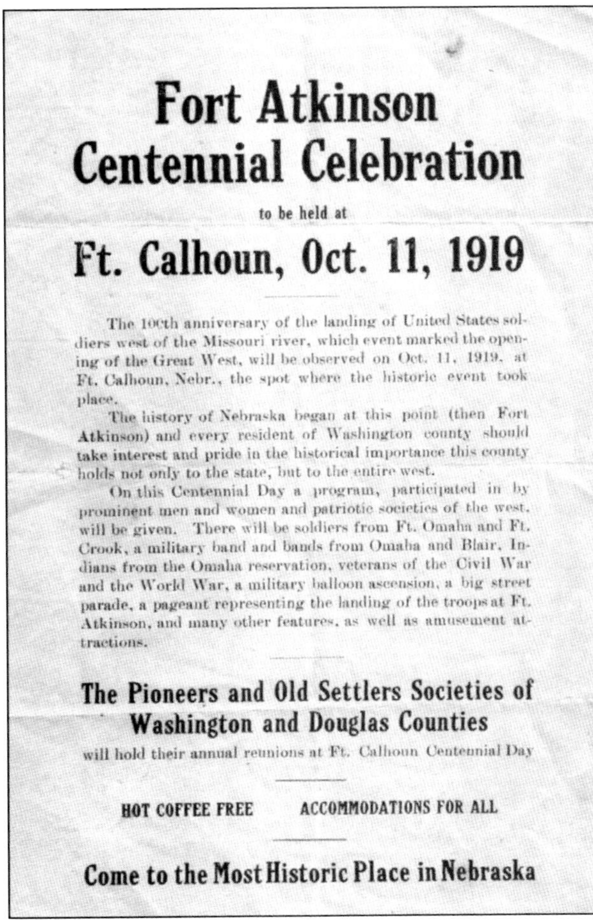

Fort Atkinson Centennial Celebration

to be held at

Ft. Calhoun, Oct. 11, 1919

The 100th anniversary of the landing of United States soldiers west of the Missouri river, which event marked the opening of the Great West, will be observed on Oct. 11, 1919, at Ft. Calhoun, Nebr., the spot where the historic event took place.

The history of Nebraska began at this point (then Fort Atkinson) and every resident of Washington county should take interest and pride in the historical importance this county holds not only to the state, but to the entire west.

On this Centennial Day a program, participated in by prominent men and women and patriotic societies of the west, will be given. There will be soldiers from Ft. Omaha and Ft. Crook, a military band and bands from Omaha and Blair, Indians from the Omaha reservation, veterans of the Civil War and the World War, a military balloon ascension, a big street parade, a pageant representing the landing of the troops at Ft. Atkinson, and many other features, as well as amusement attractions.

The Pioneers and Old Settlers Societies of Washington and Douglas Counties

will hold their annual reunions at Ft. Calhoun Centennial Day

HOT COFFEE FREE **ACCOMMODATIONS FOR ALL**

Come to the Most Historic Place in Nebraska

In 1919, a celebration was held in Fort Calhoun to commemorate the centennial of the fort's founding. This flyer announcing the event appealed to the patriotic spirit of Washington County's residents, who "should take pride and interest" at the historical importance the site held for the state and the country. It declared Fort Atkinson "the Most Historic Place in Nebraska." (Washington County Museum.)

The parade up the yet unpaved Main Street of Fort Calhoun included bands, floats, and marching units. This view of it, looking south, shows a War Veterans float and covered wagons passing the Louis Clasen blacksmith shop (sign at right) and the Warline livery stable on the corner of Fourteenth Street. (Washington County Museum.)

Pictured is a War Veterans float bedecked with flags of the world honoring the soldiers from Fort Calhoun who had fought in the Great War, which had ended only a year before. Units of military veterans from Fort Crook and Fort Omaha marched in the parade. There was also a unit of Civil War veterans, men who at that point were in their 70s and 80s. (Washington County Museum.)

The large plaster sculptures of a buffalo and mounted Indian chief were another part of the spectacle; they were specially created for the event. The Indian was placed at the south entrance of town to welcome visitors. After the celebration, they were moved to the town park where, sadly, they were melted by the rain. (Washington County Museum.)

A pageant was the principal event of the day. Players reenacted the first arrival of the Yellowstone Expedition at the Council Bluff in 1819. Posing for this photograph before a painted river panorama with steamboat are hunters/scouts, infantrymen, and officers Colonel Atkinson (on left) and Major Long. The attempt at period uniforms is a good one, and the pageant represents the first living history effort at the fort site. (Washington County Museum.)

The celebration collected a good amount of money from sales of souvenirs and refreshments and from contributions toward the event's expenses. A special Fort Atkinson Centennial coin was minted, with interesting art deco lettering. It sold quite well. Altogether, the celebration took in significantly more money than was required to mount it.

The most noteworthy personage attending that day was Col. B. W. Atkinson. Grandson of Henry Atkinson and fresh from the battlefields of Europe, he spoke and donated a portrait of his father to Fort Calhoun. Here he (left) is pictured with Col. L. S. Townsend (center) of the 6th Infantry and Capt. C. E. Adams (right), commander in chief of the Grand Army of the Republic, a Civil War veterans group. (Washington County Museum.)

On August 18, 1927, another commemoration was held. This one was for the 100th anniversary of the fort's closing. The Omaha chapter of the Daughters of the American Revolution used the occasion to proudly dedicate the 30-foot-high flagpole set in a brick and concrete base. In this rare *Omaha Sun* newspaper event image, all the DAR members stand tall below corn growing on the site. (Washington County Museum.)

Maj. D. T. Grubbs, an officer from Fort Omaha, delivered an address that officers of the 6th Infantry, now stationed at Jefferson Barracks, Missouri, helped him prepare. He called Fort Atkinson "the most westerly army post in the United States" and an important link that "did so much toward the settlement of the great Northwest." (Washington County Museum.)

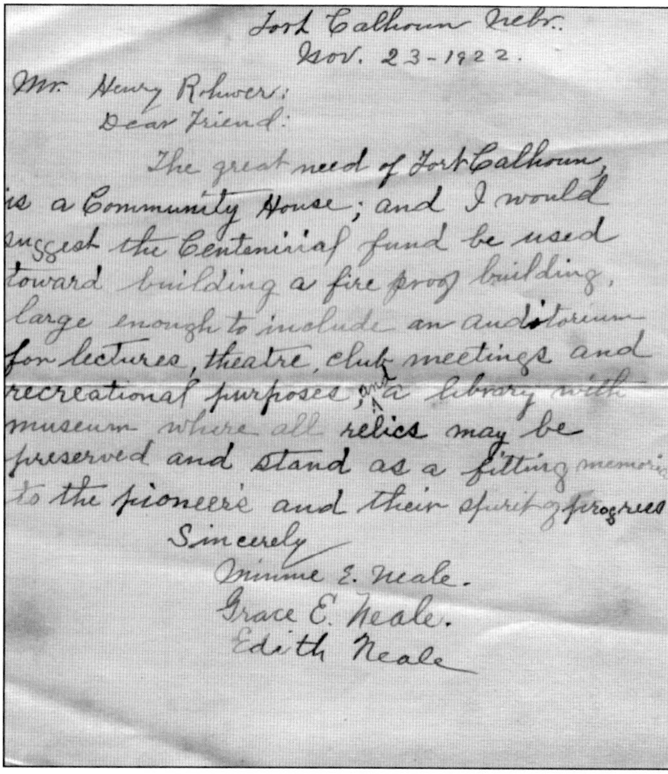

Fort Calhoun Nebr.
Nov. 23-1922.

Mr. Henry Rohwer:
Dear Friend:

The great need of Fort Calhoun is a Community House; and I would suggest the Centennial fund be used toward building a fire proof building, large enough to include an auditorium for lectures, theatre, club meetings and recreational purposes, and a library with museum where all relics may be preserved and stand as a fitting memorial to the pioneers and their spirit of progress.

Sincerely
Minnie E. Neale.
Grace E. Neale.
Edith Neale

The Neale (pronounced "Neal") sisters, lifelong residents of Fort Calhoun, were amongst those of the early group zealously struggling to preserve the fort. Their 1922 letter to George Rohwer, chairman of the effort, suggests that the excess funds garnered from the centennial celebration be used to create a combined meeting hall and museum for relics as "a fitting memorial" for the fort. (Washington County Museum.)

In 1937, the Washington County Museum was established in the vacated Fort Calhoun Bank building using the extra centennial money. Additional funding for it was achieved by the Washington County Historical Society, created after the 1919 celebration with the help of Granddaddy Woods. It was the first official place to display artifacts from the fort grounds. (Washington County Museum.)

Along with the pageant, Mrs. Ernest L. Sibert (left), regent of the Omaha chapter of the Daughters of the American Revolution, and Mrs. J. C. Strain, Nebraska DAR regent, rededicated a Lewis and Clark memorial—a 7-ton rock with a plaque that was, at the time, believed to mark the meeting spot. It had been erected at Fort Calhoun 50 years before on the centennial of the meeting. (Washington County Museum.)

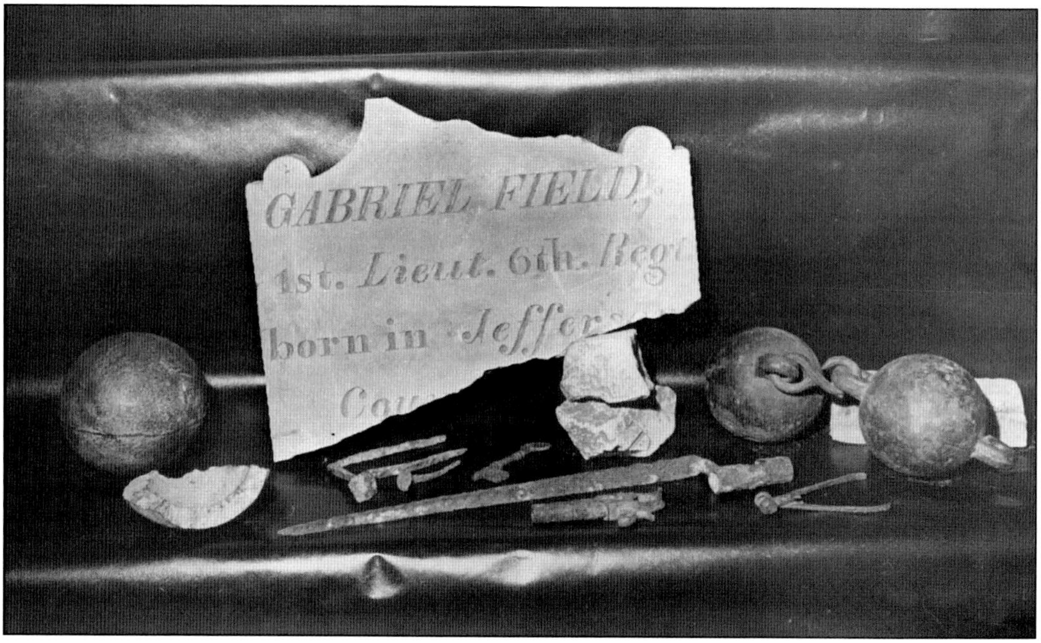

John Rathjen, who farmed land north of the fort, plowed up a large piece of headstone bearing the name Gabriel Field in 1955. Lieutenant Field was known to have been stationed at the fort, and it was now also known that he had died there. Rathjen turned the stone over to the Washington County Museum, where it is still on prominent display. (Washington County Museum.)

Over the years, the whole fort site was brought under cultivation. Debris was thrown into the old building depressions to level the area. Finally, little remained to proclaim the fort's past existence but the solitary DAR marker and flagpole that were visited occasionally by tourists and locals over the years, such as Marilyn (née Jipp) Jones in 1955. (Washington County Museum.)

In hopes that fort remains could be proven to exist before they were wiped away, the Nebraska State Historical Society mounted a dig in 1956. Archeologist Marvin Kivett (left) and his team could only excavate areas not under cultivation; this meant the land along the bluff edge, above and below the hill, along with additional excavation on the south wall. The south wall was still beneath farm buildings.

Kivett's investigation succeeded in locating the main outline of the fort. More importantly, he excavated some of the actual fortification cellars and foundations. A cellar is seen here in the south half of the east barracks. Holes for cellar posts are visible, and charring evidence from a fire was found, along with iron strap hinges.

Much of what was found proved to be substantial features. An especially impressive one was a brick-walled cellar, with all four walls still standing. As seen in this photograph, the solid walls were several bricks thick. Evidence of sophisticated lath and plaster interior finishing walls were found, along with a wealth of artifacts.

The excavations yielded up a wide variety of artifacts, giving more evidence of the complex and sophisticated life at the old fort. Visible here is a rare iron pike poll point uncovered on the brick-walled basement floor. It was identified as a spontoon, a spear-like weapon carried by officers. Remains of an officer's sword blade and still-gilded handle section were also found. (Washington County Museum.)

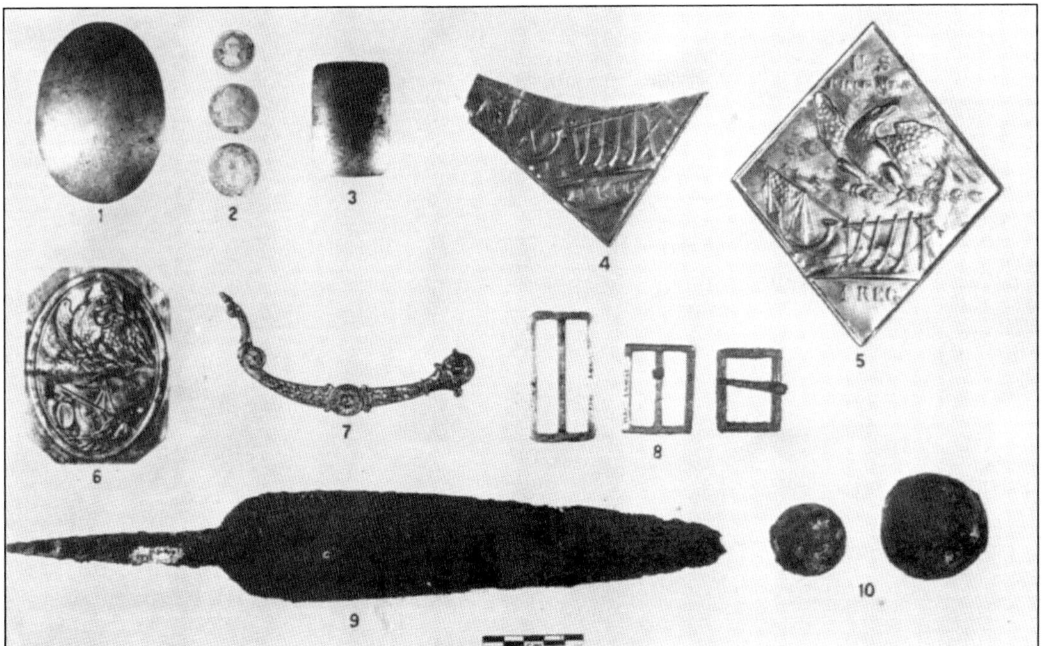

Here the pike point (9) is displayed along with a cross-belt plate (1), Spanish coins (2), a belt buckle (3), part of a rifleman's cap plate with a reproduction (4 and 5), infantry cap plate (6), a sword handle part (7), buckles (8), and small cannon shot (10). These artifacts are strong and striking evidence of the large military presence at the fort site. (Kivett.)

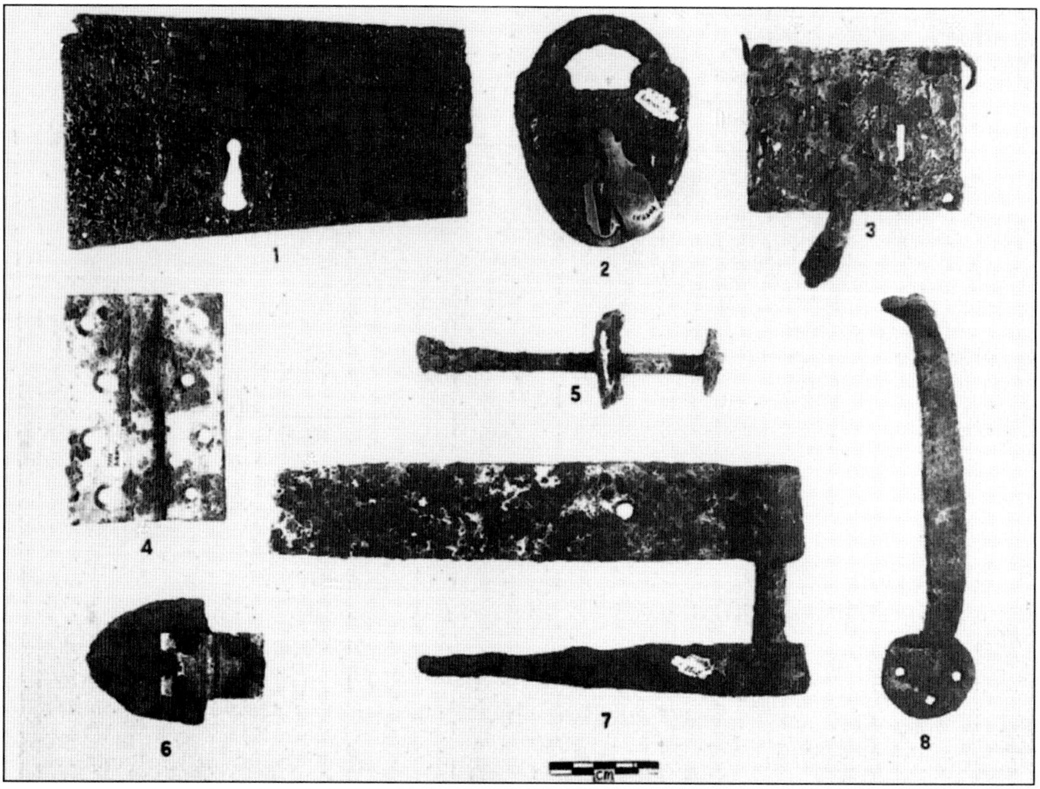

The many artifacts found included locks (1–3), hinges (4), and hardware (5-8) produced by the fort's own blacksmiths. Newspapers praised the dig as verifying the site of America's most important western outpost. Marvin Kivett made the point that this was a site predating by over three decades the beginnings of pioneer settlement in the Nebraska territories. (Kivett.)

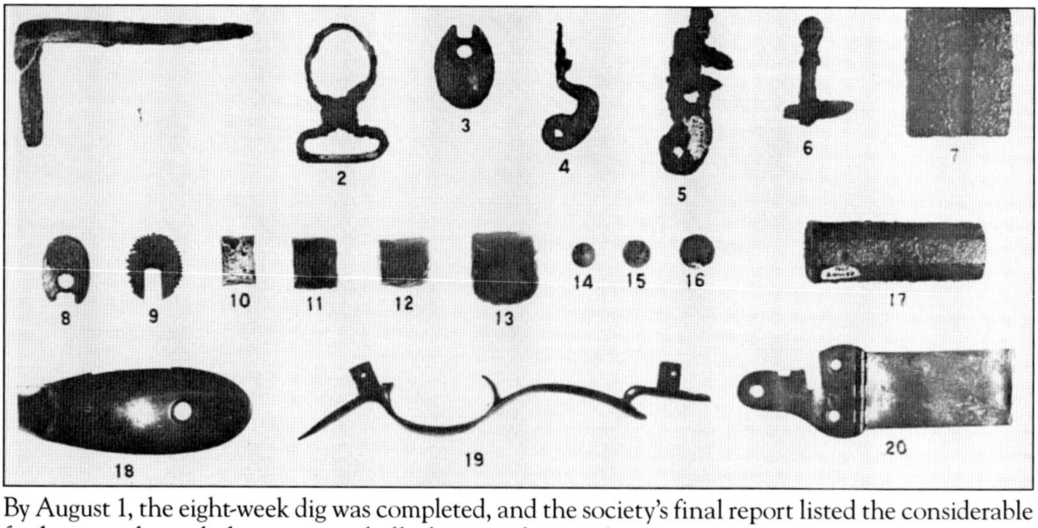

By August 1, the eight-week dig was completed, and the society's final report listed the considerable findings made, including cannon balls, buttons from military uniforms and firearm parts, tools, and accessories (1–20)—all current during the War of 1812. The fort's exact location was a proven reality now. Its value as an important historical site took on a new significance and drew important new attention. (Kivett.)

Three

Saving the Site

The new archaeological effort was successful in rekindling the public's interest in rescuing this precious place. It received enough attention that U.S. senator Roman Hruska secured $10,000 in federal cash to finance archaeological work at the old fort.

This amount was matched by the Nebraska State Historical Society, and two more digs were conducted in 1960 and 1961. These investigations focused on identifying more barracks foundations and structures beyond the barracks walls, including the blacksmith's and armorers' shop.

Publicity about the digs and open houses held on the site gained even more public enthusiasm for preserving the remains, and by 1961 a promotional group was being organized. It would be called the Fort Atkinson Foundation, a coalition of the interested and influential from Fort Calhoun, Washington County, Omaha, and across the state. Its purpose was to preserve Fort Atkinson and raise funds to purchase the site. In 1961, the foundation took out an option to buy the 144 acres of farmland on which the fort had stood. Half of the asking price of $75,000 would be paid by the Nebraska State Game and Parks Commission. The foundation set out on a two-year effort to raise the other half.

A massive fund-raising drive was launched. It involved individuals, companies, organizations, and agencies from Nebraska and around the country. A special Omaha Committee for Fort Atkinson was created for the purpose. Print and electronic media played their part, and brochures, a television special, celebrations, commemorative items, and personal appeals were utilized. A special column in the *Omaha World-Herald* reported on the drive's progress weekly, assuring the public that every contribution would be acknowledged—and it was. By the end of 1962, the fund was over the top. Thousands of people had contributed, ranging from schoolchildren donating pennies, nickels, and dimes to business firms and individuals giving up to $1,000.

In 1963, the property's ownership was transferred to the Fort Atkinson Foundation, which, in turn, handed the land over to the State of Nebraska for $1. The fort's site was now safe. The foundation had succeeded. The foundations were secure.

Three influential Nebraska politicians were instrumental in seeking backing to preserve the site. U.S. senator Carl Curtis (left) initiated an effort to force the federal government to recognize the fort's historical importance. Sen. Roman Hruska (center) and Congressman Glen Cunningham (right) joined him in the fight. Bills were introduced in the house and senate to have the National Park Service designate the fort as a national historical site.

Historical Site status depended on a thorough archeological investigation of the fort's remains. Roman Hruska obtained $10,000 in federal funding. Matched by the Nebraska State Historical Society, this was enough for two new digs. The first one began in the summer of 1960. The crew wielded spades to begin with before using whisk brooms and trowels to remove earth an inch at a time.

Because the site was still in private ownership, the dig was again confined to areas not farmed (crops can be seen at top). Here a crew continues work on the east barracks wall along the bluff's edge. They uncovered more barracks basements and foundations. This photograph also shows the H-shaped limestone base of a large, double-sided fireplace.

An even more impressive and most unusual find was an 18-foot stretch of brick walkway. It was uncovered just outside the southern wall of the east barracks line. It represents yet another fort first for Nebraska—the first stretch of paved sidewalk. It and the above features were reburied, and they still exist beneath the sod along the bluff's edge. (Blair *Enterprise*.)

An important find in this dig was the large H-shaped fireplace base. Built of limestone from a nearby quarry, it was located in the south half of the east barracks line. It is the best-preserved example of a double-sided fireplace base to be found at the fort. Preserved today under a protective concrete cover, it provided valuable information for the accurate reconstruction of the new fort's fireplaces.

Most exciting to the public was the location of the Fort Atkinson smithy, a significant structure outside the main walls and some 30 feet by 40 feet in size. It was at an unexpected location at the base of the bluff. Marvin Kivett, considered an archaeological Sherlock Holmes by his young assistants, found the spot somewhat miraculously. He just dug a little test hole, and there it was.

The blacksmith's shop was a veritable treasure trove of artifacts, yielding up a pile of slag, ox or mule shoes, chain links, a file, broken glass, and part of an oarlock or pitchfork, plus a large iron broadhead axe. Here archeology crewman John Rosenburg sits in the excavation to hold up the just-uncovered axe head for examination. (Nebraska State Historical Society.)

Although the thought might seem a bit distasteful, one of the richest spots for discovering artifacts can be an outhouse. Such places were a convenient disposal point for broken or worn-out objects, and many interesting finds—cutlery, ceramics, razors, knives, bottles, pipes, even toothbrushes—were made there. This one was northeast of the barracks quadrangle, near the bluff edge.

As always, every effort was made to turn this expedition into some positive publicity and gain support for saving the fort. There was to be an open house at the dig, with visitors gathering in the Fort Calhoun town park to be escorted to the excavations. This group is seen examining a cellar near the bluff edge on the east barracks line.

The hundreds who visited the site were treated to an amazing stroke of luck. A large metal hood that had crowned a forge in the original smithy, crushed but intact, was unearthed by the diggers at the height of the visiting hours. Here the enthralled crowd listens to Marvin Kivett describe the dramatic find brought back into the light of day after 130 years.

A Prospectus For

Fort Atkinson

PUBLISHED BY

FORT ATKINSON FOUNDATIO

Fort Calhoun, Nebraska

". . . crossroads of raw histor

By 1961, a Fort Atkinson Foundation was organized to buy and preserve the site. The Nebraska State Game and Parks Commission committed to supplying half of the $75,000 needed, and the foundation set out to raise the rest. A first step in the fund-raising was this brochure, created by *World-Herald* editor and foundation member Maxwell Coffey. Its cover showed the outline of the fort's site marked on an aerial photograph. The inside pages gave a brief fort history, pictured some of the artifacts found, and asked the public to contribute toward rescuing Fort Atkinson, a "crossroads of raw history."

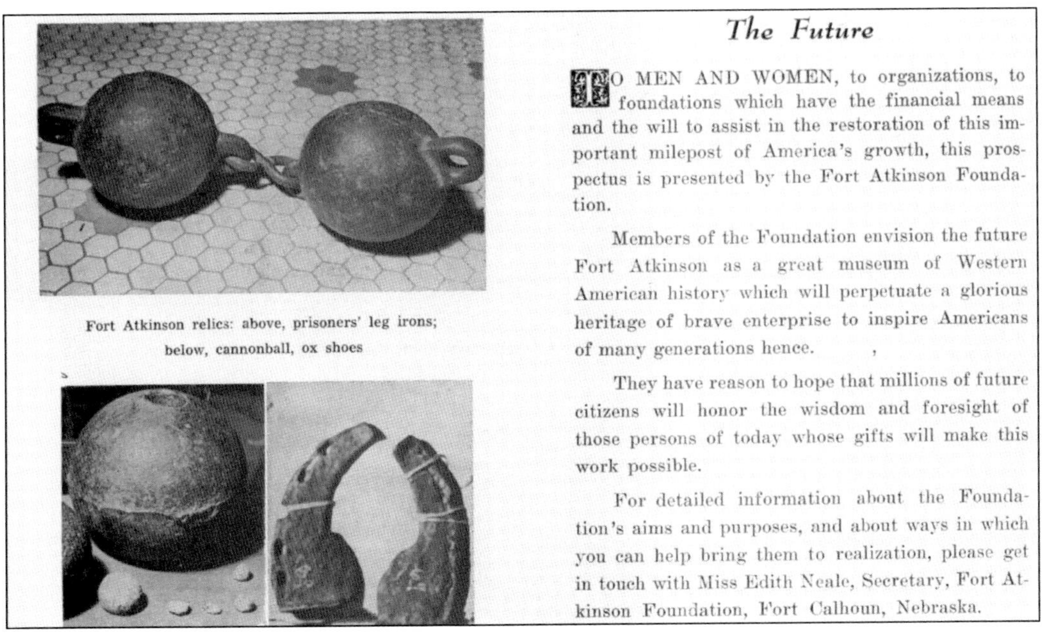

Fort Atkinson relics: above, prisoners' leg irons; below, cannonball, ox shoes

The Future

TO MEN AND WOMEN, to organizations, to foundations which have the financial means and the will to assist in the restoration of this important milepost of America's growth, this prospectus is presented by the Fort Atkinson Foundation.

Members of the Foundation envision the future Fort Atkinson as a great museum of Western American history which will perpetuate a glorious heritage of brave enterprise to inspire Americans of many generations hence.

They have reason to hope that millions of future citizens will honor the wisdom and foresight of those persons of today whose gifts will make this work possible.

For detailed information about the Foundation's aims and purposes, and about ways in which you can help bring them to realization, please get in touch with Miss Edith Neale, Secretary, Fort Atkinson Foundation, Fort Calhoun, Nebraska.

Another, and most significant, first for the fort came in 1961. This printed photograph from the *Fort Calhoun Chronicle* is the only existing image of the very first dedication of a Nebraska Historical Marker, now a common sight across the state. It was erected beside the Washington County Museum (marker under flag at right) and commemorates the vital part the fort played 30 years before the organization of the territory.

In late 1961, the Fort Atkinson Foundation prepared for a major campaign to raise the required funds to buy the site's farmland and preserve the fort. Many movers and shakers of Washington County served on the foundation. Seen here are, from left to right, (first row) Genevieve Slader, Catherine Frahm, and Edith Neale; (second row) H. Lyle Guyer, Luther Monke, Harold Swanson, Ed Lorenzen, George Rohwer, Pierce Allen, and J. Merton Kuhr. (Washington County Museum.)

The early foundation's most notable figure was Edith Neale, who also donated the land for Omaha's Neale Woods Nature Center. A teacher and writer, she devoted much of her life to Fort Atkinson's preservation. When the Washington County Museum was created, she helped organize it and served as its curator until 1976. Here she is seen with Fort Calhoun pupils, from left to right, Peggy Foral, Anne Boham, and Rozanne Seidel. (Washington County Museum.)

Another NSHS dig took place in 1961. John Garrett (fourth from left) was supervisor of his crews' archeological effort. This time the purpose was to learn more about fort features like the blacksmith's and the armorer's shops and to excavate more of the south and east barracks lines. At an open house accompanying the dig, hundreds jammed into a tent to hear Garrett describe the displays of artifacts found. (Nebraska State Historical Society.)

Famed Nebraska novelist Mari Sandoz was another fort promoter. She spoke glowingly and wistfully of Fort Atkinson, calling it "the most romantic, by far, of western posts," a jumping off point for adventurers, and the first true frontier army fort, "setting the tone" for those that followed. She said that Fort Atkinson could be the inspiration for one of her own novels. It's too bad she never wrote it.

In 1962, the major fund-raising campaign was launched, beginning on Sunday, February 18. The *Omaha World-Herald*'s "Magazine of the Midlands" for that day had as its cover a striking painting by *World-Herald* artist John Svoboda entitled, *Where Two Hunters Meet*. It depicted the fort's barracks atop the Council Bluff in the background. Inside was a two-page piece by fort friend and *OWH* editor Max Coffey.

All contributions will be acknowledged in the news columns of The World-Herald.

Today's contributors:

Omaha World-Herald	$1,000.00
J. M. McDonald Foundation, Inc., Hastings	1,000.00
O'Hanlon Family, Blair	1,000.00
Bertha Neale, Omaha	500.00
Dora Klindt, Fort Calhoun	500.00
Fort Atkinson Post, No. 348, American Legion, Fort Calhoun	300.00
Edith Neale, Fort Calhoun	250.00
Grace Neale, Fort Calhoun	250.00
Mr. and Mrs. Frank Latenser, Omaha	100.00
A. R. Owens, Loup City	50.00
Guyer and Hansen, Blair	37.50
Winifred O. Parr, Long Beach, Cal.	25.00
P. C. Hyson, Omaha	25.00
Blair Commercial Travelers Booster Club, Blair	15.00
R. R. and Salma Hammond, Bushnell	5.00
Rev. P. C. Jensen, Blair	5.00
Mrs. Harold J. Way, Lincoln	3.00
Fourth Grade Pupils, Bennington School	2.62
Robert Lee Hill, Omaha	2.00
Total	**$5,070.12**

The *Omaha World-Herald* was an especially valuable fund-raising ally, taking the foundation project under its wing. The newspaper published biweekly articles identifying every contributor, large and small. This example article, the first one, identifies the *World-Herald*'s own contribution plus those of Edith Neale and her sisters and Frank Latenser of the renowned Omaha architectural firm. Also noted is the $2.62 collected by fourth-grade pupils.

By the summer of 1962, there was less than $9,000 left to raise. Two new promotional schemes were initiated. One of these was the minting of souvenir coins bearing the Rifle Regiment insignia. There were 5,000 of them, each to be sold for $1. They went on sale on August 3.

Booths were set up in downtown Omaha by the Omaha Junior Chamber of Congress to peddle the coins. They could also be purchased at the *World-Herald* information desk or by mail. Other "salesmen" sold coins door to door to city businesses; 200 were sold at the Omaha Stockyards, and Paxton Vierling Steel purchased 500 to promote the fort to customers all over the country.

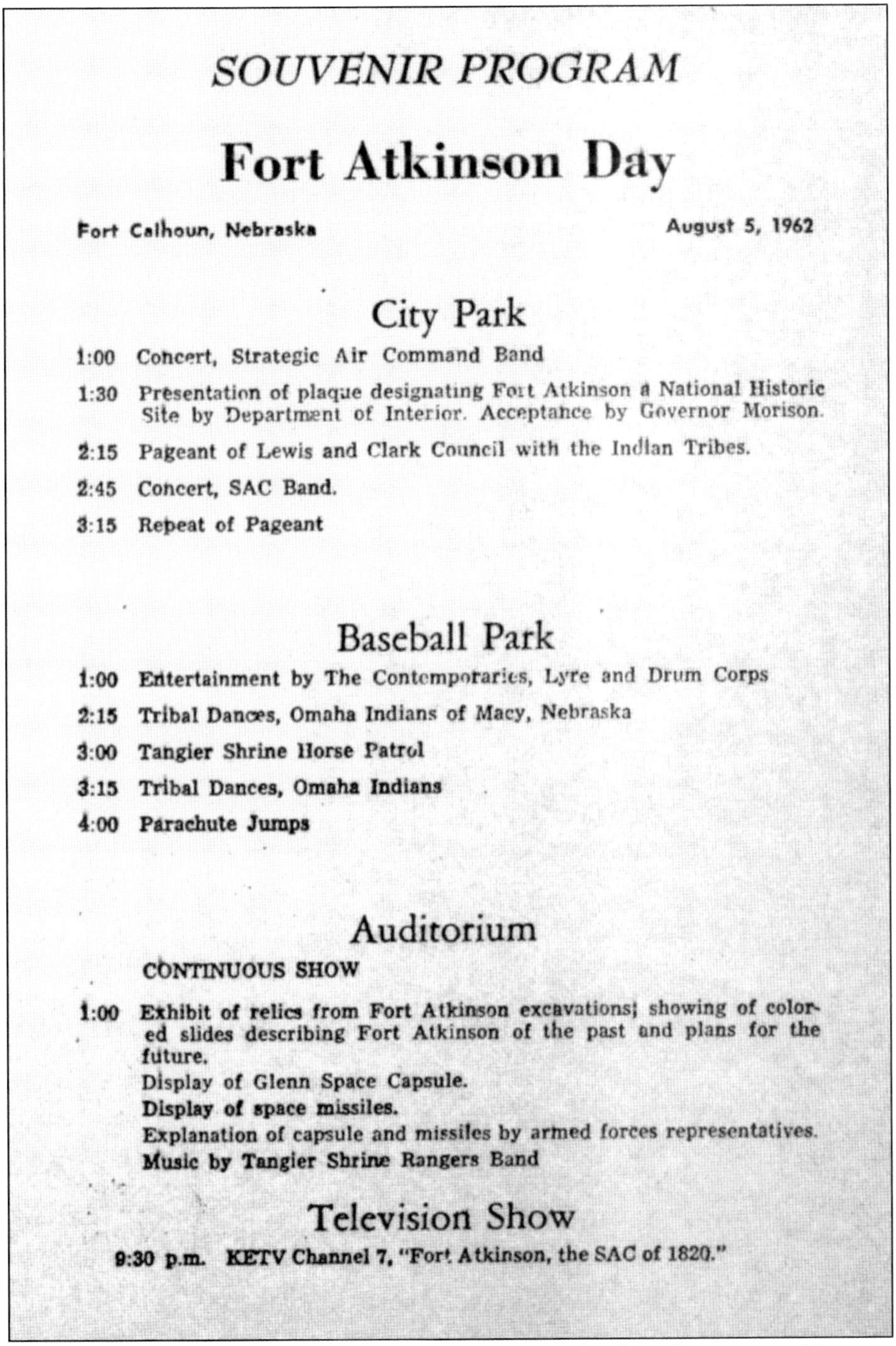
SOUVENIR PROGRAM

Fort Atkinson Day

Fort Calhoun, Nebraska **August 5, 1962**

City Park

1:00 Concert, Strategic Air Command Band

1:30 Presentation of plaque designating Fort Atkinson a National Historic Site by Department of Interior. Acceptance by Governor Morison.

2:15 Pageant of Lewis and Clark Council with the Indian Tribes.

2:45 Concert, SAC Band.

3:15 Repeat of Pageant

Baseball Park

1:00 Entertainment by The Contemporaries, Lyre and Drum Corps

2:15 Tribal Dances, Omaha Indians of Macy, Nebraska

3:00 Tangier Shrine Horse Patrol

3:15 Tribal Dances, Omaha Indians

4:00 Parachute Jumps

Auditorium

CONTINUOUS SHOW

1:00 Exhibit of relics from Fort Atkinson excavations; showing of colored slides describing Fort Atkinson of the past and plans for the future.
Display of Glenn Space Capsule.
Display of space missiles.
Explanation of capsule and missiles by armed forces representatives.
Music by Tangier Shrine Rangers Band

Television Show

9:30 p.m. KETV Channel 7, "Fort Atkinson, the SAC of 1820."

The foundation also organized a Fort Atkinson Day to raise funds and increase public awareness. Activities for the day included concerts, parachute jumps, tribal dances from the Omaha tribe, and a pageant depicting the Lewis and Clark First Council. Over 7,500 people attended the event. In addition, a show was produced by Omaha television station KETV dramatizing the history of the old fort. This was at the height of the Cold War, and it was noted that the old fort served the same purpose in safeguarding America as the modern Strategic Air Command (SAC).

The fort cause was further aided when it was granted Registered National Historical Landmark status by the National Park Service in 1962. Landmark status meant that Fort Atkinson had finally been recognized as a nationally significant historic place by the secretary of the interior because of its exceptional value in illustrating the heritage of the United States. It made the Fort Atkinson site the only place of such designation in the state of Nebraska. It was also one of only three military outposts in the Midwest with such a status.

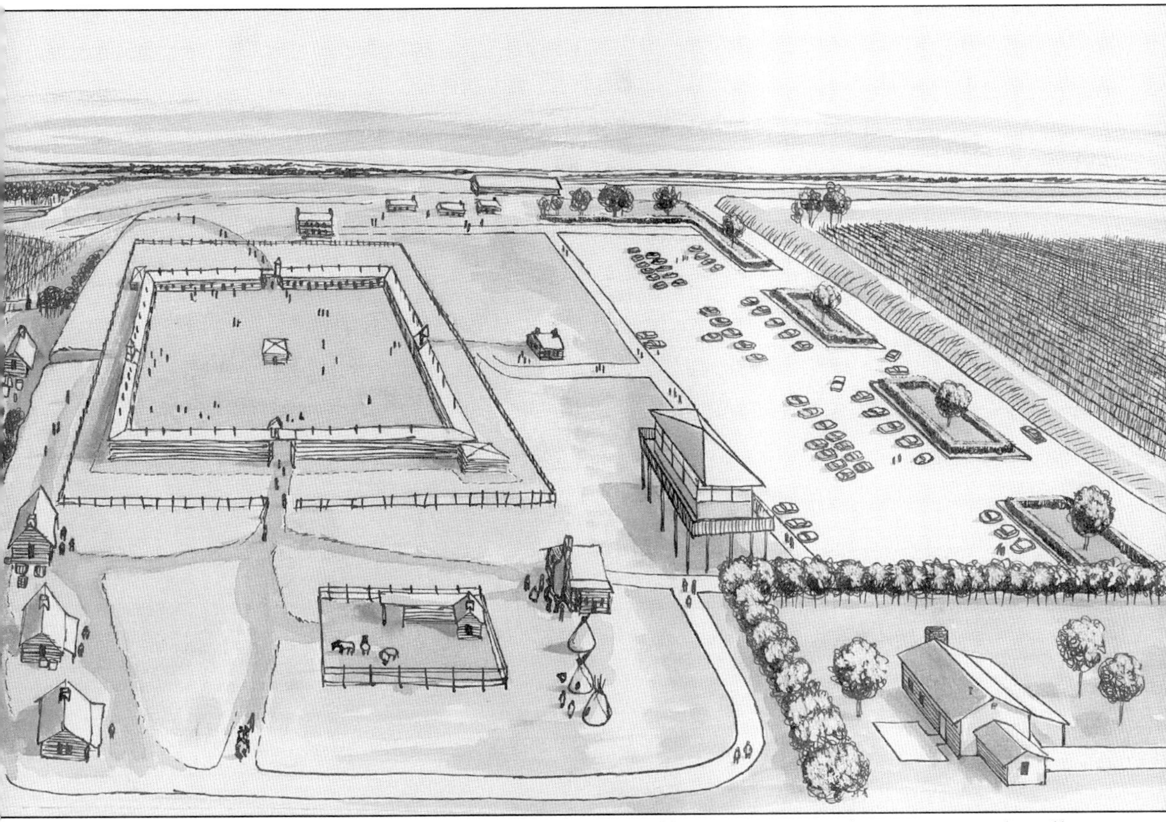

With the success of the fund-raiser in late 1962, Max Coffey wrote an article recounting the effort to save the fort and laying out its hoped-for future. This accompanying drawing by John Svoboda depicts what a restored Fort Atkinson might look like. It is intriguing to compare this rendering with what has so far actually resulted at the site (see pages 2 and 114). (*Omaha World-Herald.*)

With the site now in the hands of the Nebraska Game and Parks Commission, the entire fort could come under archaeological scrutiny. A new dig was launched by the NSHS in 1964. Investigation was carried out on the west and north barracks lines and on other buildings in those directions. Diggers uncovered the northwest bastion area (seen here looking north), revealing the palisade trench and scattered rubble from a fireplace.

There was also a first dig on the powder magazine, the last structure to stand on the grounds. This revealed what a good-sized and sturdily constructed building it was, as it had to be to contain any chance explosions. Heavy limestone footings 2.5 feet wide and 1.5 feet deep supported thick walls of heavily plastered bricks 26 feet long and 16 feet wide.

Excavation was done on what was thought to be the Council House. This large and separate building was a potentially important find. By the end of the 1964 dig, cellars and foundations had been identified on all four of the barracks lines, and more fireplace bases had been found. Also came the quite exciting find pictured—a complete chimney that had collapsed into a dirt-walled cellar.

In 1967, Col. Virgil Ney, U.S. Army, Ret., contacted the foundation. A teacher and researcher with a Ph.D. from Georgetown University, he would produce a book on the fort's early history. Entitled *The Fort on the Prairie*, it would become the principle source of information on Fort life and the bible for the future living history volunteers.

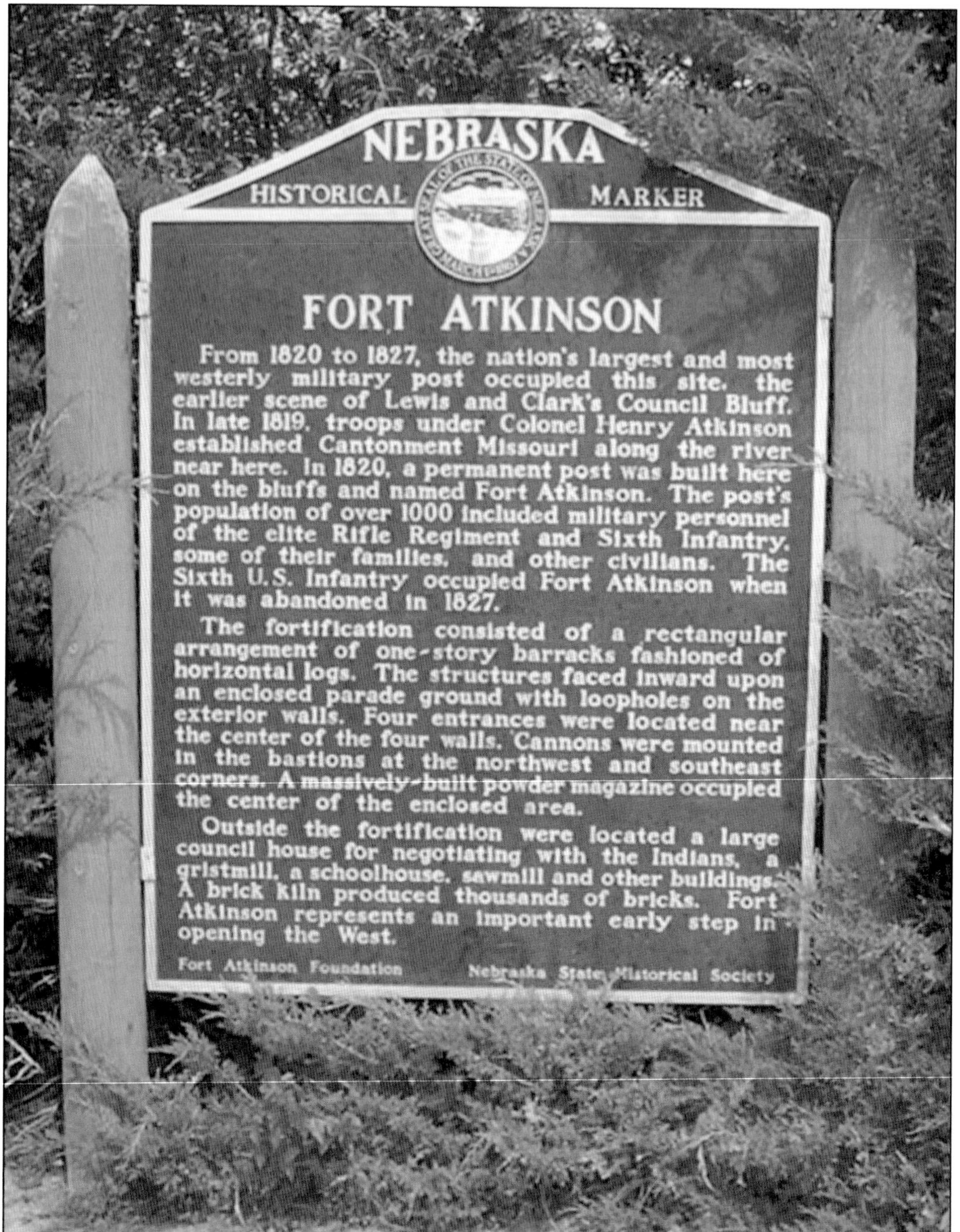

In 1967, a second Fort Atkinson marker was erected on the actual fort site. The dedication program, held on August 2, included a historic scene with portrayals of Atkinson and Leavenworth. Other events included a concert by the SAC band and another talk on archeological findings by Marvin Kivett. There was a rededication of the town's original fort marker in town. Most importantly, there was the unveiling of the new fort marker on the park grounds. It described the fort's buildings and called the site "an important early step in opening the West."

Four

Creating the Park

A real milestone year for the site was 1970. Fort Atkinson State Historical Park opened to the public. That summer there was also a new dig by the NSHS to locate the southeast bastion, originally a palisade of upended logs. With the archaeology concluded, a Nebraska Game and Parks crew erected a new bastion on the site of the old. The restoration of Fort Atkinson had actually begun.

It was the same year that the first park superintendent, Stephen Kemper, began a 20-year stint that would transform the site from an empty cornfield to a major state historical park site. Besides beginning site cleanup, one of Kemper's first duties was excavating the northwest bastion area. By Independence Day 1971, workers were setting the sharpened poles of the second palisade in its trench footings.

By June 1972, a parking lot had been created, and a new road swept northwesterly to a new entrance for the grounds. In addition, modern bathrooms now rose by the parking lot. Fort renovation was also continuing, with a west gate being constructed as a palisade of logs, helping visitors better visualize the outline and size of the fort grounds.

A temporary interpretive center with historical displays was completed by the summer of 1973. The park's crew also worked on a brick walk to connect the parking lot to the west gate. It was completed in time for the museum opening. Native grasses were planted to bring back the look of the original prairie. On the Fourth of July that year, interpreters began doing demonstrations of black powder firearms for the public, and Steve Kemper began firing off a first fort cannon he had acquired.

The dream of reconstructing the fort proper moved toward reality in 1975 with plans developed for building a first barracks section. Work began in June 1977, and by that fall the foundations for the first barracks were in place. Logs began arriving at the site the following spring, and the construction work began. By 1980, the 200-foot-long barracks building was complete. A new stage of the fort's development had arrived.

A Nebraska State Historical Society crew dug on the site in 1970 to locate the southeast bastion trench. This was in preparation for rebuilding the bastion. The dig also exposed buried elements of the west and south barracks line like stone foundations, basements, and fireplace bases. Many more artifacts were located, including Spanish coins and cannon balls. (Blair *Pilot-Tribune*.)

With the bastion location identified, Nebraska Game and Parks workers, including, from left to right, Jeff Kirkland, Les Johnson, and John Davis, worked to rebuild the log structure. A cannon within this bastion protected the south and east walls of the old fort. It is especially notable as the first structure of the original fortress to be accurately rebuilt.

With the official opening of Fort Atkinson State Historical Park in 1970, Steve Kemper was assigned as its first superintendent. Here he poses beside the park's new entrance sign. Kemper would serve as superintendent for the next 20 years, helping to develop the park and working on the reconstruction of many of the fort buildings.

A 1971 dig by the Nebraska State Historical Society also identified the northwest bastion trench. The excavation was still underway as Steve Kemper, with the help of first seasonal worker Tony Christensen, erected the second bastion by hand. Defining this diagonal corner allowed visitors to more easily visualize the fort's dimensions. Archaeologist Carl Jones (by truck) supervises John Slader (foreground). There are a white trailer and historical marker behind Jones. (*Omaha World-Herald.*)

To further define the size and outline of the fort, the gateways into the quadrangle were next identified for reconstruction. The west gateway was the first, erected in 1972. This photograph looks to the southeast, with the flagpole framed by the opening and the far, southwest corner bastion visible behind the trees to the left.

By 1973, with a new parking lot finished, an elegantly curving brick walk was laid connecting it to the west gateway. The bricks were salvaged from old Highway 73, running between Fort Calhoun and Omaha. The look of the walk purposely recalled that original fort sidewalk unearthed during the 1960 dig.

A major development came for the park in 1973 when the first interpretive center was opened in this trailer at the northeast corner of the parking lot. It contained a welcome and information center for visitors and a museum whose displays illustrated the history of the fort with graphics, paintings, and many artifacts.

Steve Kemper labored through the winter with local craftsmen and park staff to create displays for the new visitors center. It was the first time that some of the plethora of artifacts discovered over the years could actually be displayed on the site of the old fort. Kemper is seen in this Blair *Enterprise* photograph putting final touches to a display of ironwork produced by the fort blacksmiths.

The first cannon at the Fort, dubbed "Little Richard," was an antique two-pounder barrel mounted on a handmade carriage built in the park's workshop. Its debut performance was at the July Fourth celebration in 1973. These photographs from a *Ft. Calhoun Chronicle* article show Steve Kemper lighting the fuse (before running) to demonstrate the new cannon with black powder and paper wadding.

In the fall of 1973, work on the county road south and west of the fort came upon the remains of a latrine and a cellar containing many artifacts. A crew from the Game and Parks Commission came in to do the archaeology. Here Steve Kemper examines a part of the excavation.

Roye Lindsay, the commission's archaeologist, led the dig. Here he examines some of the artifacts. The serrated item on the small sheet is a metal hat plate. The smaller round items are uniform buttons, including a convex pewter button with an eagle and a star. Other items include bottle, dish, and metal pieces. (Washington County Museum.)

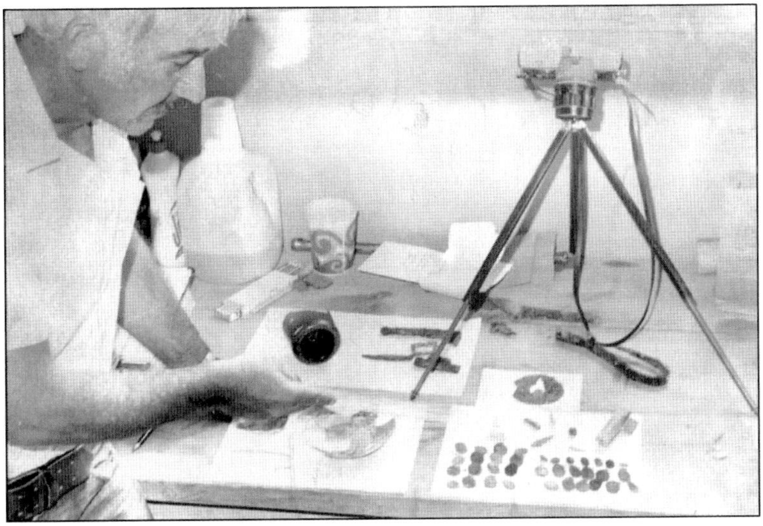

This 1974 aerial photograph of the fort site lays out the progress made in developing the state historical park during its first years of operation. The paved entrance road (top) welcomed the public to the new parking lot, restrooms, and interpretive center. The bricked path led visitors to the west gateway (center, near flagpole) and the angled corner bastions that defined the fort's outlines. (Nebraska Air National Guard.)

The most significant activity in the spring of 1975 was an extensive archaeological investigation of the west barracks line's southern half. This time the purpose was to insure that any structural evidence or artifacts had been identified and cleared. No building could be done until this was accomplished and the historical society had given approval. Here Steve Kemper and assistant superintendent John Slader clear sod for the dig.

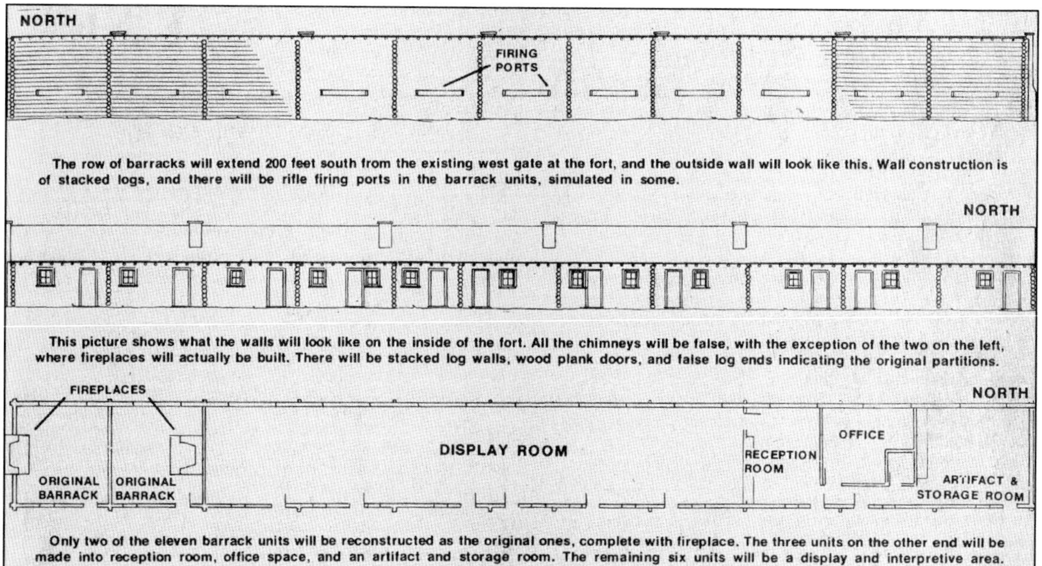

Plans for the proposed first barracks were drawn up by parks commission engineers and appeared publicly for the first time in the Blair *Pilot-Tribune* newspaper. In the original plan, a visitors center and museum were to be incorporated into the building. Only the two rooms at the left would be furnished as period replicas.

The coming American bicentennial in 1976 greatly increased the interest in black powder shooting. Area muzzle loading groups began visiting the fort and giving demonstrations to the public. In this Blair *Enterprise* photograph, from left to right, Rod Olsen of Kennard, Gordy Whitcomb of Fremont, and Dean Slader of Valley show visitors how a flintlock works. The tepee behind them belongs to Bill Ihm of Davy.

For the American bicentennial, Fort Calhoun staged a major celebration in the town. As with past festivities, this included concerts, displays, a parade, a balloon ascension, and carriage rides. The celebration was very successful and would begin the tradition of an annual Fort Calhoun Heritage Days that would continue through the 1990s. This parade float celebrates Fort Atkinson being the site of Nebraska's first school.

The bicentennial celebration was a cooperative effort of the town and Fort Atkinson SHP. In addition to activities in Fort Calhoun, visitors were driven to the park in carriages. Here they toured the site, examined preparations for the barracks reconstruction, and watched period black powder demonstrations. This view is southwest, past the bastion to the west gate and trailer.

A Bicentennial Wagon Train, which made a ceremonial trek across the United States in 1976, stopped overnight at the fort site in late April. There was a welcoming program and party held in the parking lot by the visitor center. Steve Kemper, always helpful, organized townsfolk to feed the trekkers.

The year 1977 was a particularly significant milestone for the fort. By the fall, the foundations for the first barracks construction were in place. A floor slab covered the original base of the building, and a single brick, double-sided fireplace with tall chimney arose, elegant but as yet alone, from near the southern end. John Slader can be seen moving blocks in for further work.

Building began in June 1978. Workers from Lok-N-Logs (in the hats at right), which had supplied the timber, trained the parks crew for a week; then they were on their own. As Steve Kemper puts it, "We were in the fort building business!" Seen here from left to right are (first row) Steve Corrigan, Lem Binkley, and Jerry Farber; (second row) Dean Sandahl, Bob Slechta, Ronald "Rusty" Adams, Kemper, John Slader, Brian Gage, and two unidentified Lok-N-Logs workers.

This small crew with little equipment and antiquated tools is seen taking on an arduous and most unusual task—to construct a 20-foot-by-200-foot structure one log at a time. Still, the work went rapidly, with the walls rising steadily through June. Each log added represents about a foot of wall height.

Each log was shaped and notched by hand with axes and saws. It was then was hoisted and set into the walls. Overlapping notches (seen here) tied the logs together lengthwise, and metal pins secured them in place. Steve Kemper (right) oversees the work by John Slader (on the ground); Jerry Farber and Brian Gage (second to right) are astride the wall.

By midsummer 1978, the crew had reached a height of 9 feet on the walls, finishing the basic construction of the barrack's lower, rectangular section. The inner wall (in foreground), with its windows and doors, was at full height. The outer wall had to rise another 5 feet to accommodate the sloping roof. Kemper (right) and Brian Gage are seen attaching the top log.

The additional 5 feet brought the crew a new challenge. The loader arm of their tractor could not reach high enough to place the top tiers of logs. Their solution was to place these logs one by one on a scaffold in the back of a pickup, run them in close, and then place them by hand. Here Slader drives the loader, while Kemper and crew maneuver a log into place.

Next the crew constructed heavy, triangular braces atop the interior walls and attached the outer 5 feet of logs to these. They then constructed trusses, 102 of them, gluing and nailing half-inch plywood gussets on both sides of each to secure the joints, attaching them to the log structure with a whole lot more notching.

With the log walls erected, finishing work could begin. Chinking crews began to fill the gaps between tiers with a specially prepared chinking material. Thousands of pounds of this would be used. Other crews worked to complete the truss work so that roofing could begin the following season. The basic structure was complete by summer's end.

With the barrack's log walls fully erected, chinking underway, and roofs added to the southernmost rooms, Fort Atkinson entered a new era. It could now more completely fulfill the function that has always been the park's most vital purpose—to educate the public. Here Steve Kemper tells an enthralled group of Omaha students about the fort history as they look eastward toward the partly constructed barracks.

Kemper is seen standing by that first double fireplace, now enclosed by the southernmost barracks room. He regales another student group from Fort Calhoun Elementary School. With work still underway, he was not only able to interpret the fort's original life but to explain the construction techniques being used to restore it.

June 1979 saw Kemper's park crew stripping the sod from the site of the northern end of the west wall in preparation for further archaeological work. This summer's dig was based on the expectation that work would go on past the southwest barracks to the rebuilding of the entire west wall. The dig crew was lead by Gayle Carlson and Tim Hajek of the state historical society. However, as funds for laborers were short for the society, Nebraska Game and Parks provided a party of diggers to help in the six-week dig including, in this shot, Kemper (seated at rear, second from right) and Slader (standing in excavation, second from left). In the upper center of the dig, a worker can be seen standing in a cellar being excavated. To the left are the screens used to sift every bucket of earth for artifacts. Hajek (in foreground) is seen keeping track of progress on a chart of the dig.

This photograph shows the archaeology team working its way toward the north bastion at the rear. The excavation method is typical of such digs. The ground is carefully dug out in 5-foot squares, each square identified by a number. Artifacts are collected and labeled by the square's number. The raised mounds are simply corner markers for identification purposes.

Artifacts from the dig were laid out on display trays such as this one for the archaeologists to inspect. This collection provides a good example of the typical findings made during the fort excavations. It includes buttons, marbles, buckles, hinges, keys, and pieces of pottery. Such items turn up in the fort's sod to this day. (*Fort Calhoun Chronicle*.)

With some park personnel assisting in the excavation and sifting on the dig, work on finishing the barracks was slowed. Even so, by August, six of the rooms had been roofed and at least partly chinked. Here the first three rooms have been fully chinked and have had doors and windows framed; they only await shingling.

Also by August, the archaeological investigation was nearing the north end of the east barracks line and the bastion. John Slader (left), Brian Gage (center), and Jerry Farber are seen working to install the interior ceiling beams for the last room of the first barracks line. Beyond them, others are continuing to dig and sift the last few feet of the excavation.

Publicity from the continuing reconstruction and that year's dig brought deserved and welcome new attention to the fort. A film crew from Nebraska Educational Television (cameraman Rick Hagberg seen here) shot a documentary on the rebuilding and the archaeology, interviewing park personnel Kemper and Slader and archaeologists Hajek and Carlson.

U.S. representative John Cavanaugh of Nebraska's 2nd District (encompassing Omaha) also visited the fort grounds in the summer of 1979. Park superintendent Kemper (at right) took the congressman (center, in white pants) and his entourage on a tour of the new buildings and dig site. Cavanaugh, like many Nebraska politicians before and after, was a strong supporter of developing this important historical spot.

By 1980, the historical park was becoming recognized as a valuable educational experience. The 200-foot-long barracks structure, lovingly re-created and accurate to the period, was now complete. Steve Kemper, garbed in an infantryman's uniform, was the fort's first living history for the visitors, showing off the new barracks rooms and enthusiastically interpreting the fort's past. (*Fort Calhoun Chronicle.*)

The finished rooms were furnished with period-correct handmade bunk beds, tables, and benches, the first of many such pieces to be built right at the fort. Kemper was also fitted-out in the remarkably authentic uniform of a 6th Infantry private. This earns the park superintendent credit for being the first person to interpret at Fort Atkinson in proper period military dress. (*Fort Calhoun Chronicle.*)

Five

Resurrecting the Fort

As the newly completed barracks began drawing greater numbers of visitors to Fort Atkinson, Steve Kemper began developing the living history interpretation. His ambitious plans for building a program were already in the preliminary stages. In fact, since the early 1970s, Steve Kemper had been drawing black powder and buckskinner groups to the site to entertain the public. Now, members of those groups were taking on the more specific personas of the fort's era. One of the first interpretations was that of the fort's blacksmiths, performed open-air with a portable anvil and forge. Others joined the tiny group of fort players as spinners, trappers, and early explorers.

The fort's reconstruction was continuing as well. A foundation was laid for the north end of the west wall, and work began to build the rest of the entire barracks line. With a surplus of logs from this construction, Kemper approached the blacksmiths with the idea of having them build an armorers' shop. They agreed and went to work on a structure that would take three years to complete. When the north end of the west barracks was completed, work began on the construction of the entire south barracks line.

This decade was a record one for building at the park. In 1986, the armorers' shop was completed. More importantly, a permanent, modern, state-of-the-art visitors center was opened. It housed a welcoming lobby, interpretive spaces, animated displays, brick murals, and a theater. Another significant structure, the Council House, was also erected, and work began on a trapper's cabin.

More interpreters joined the fort's living history. Most significant was the Discovery Corps, a group interpreting the Lewis and Clark Expedition. Some of their members would form the official interpretive program yet to come. By the late 1980s, several of them were already portraying soldiers at the fort, adding to a growing list of scenarios, including spinners, blacksmiths, gunsmiths, a cooper, a carpenter, and fur traders.

The end of the 1980s saw one other major change. John Slader replaced Steve Kemper as park superintendent. It would be his responsibility to continue the fort's development and create an official living history program.

The first volunteer interpreters at Fort Atkinson were buckskinner and black powder enthusiasts like these members of the Fort Atkinson Muzzleloaders. Steve Kemper invited them for yearly winter encampments and shoots on the old river channel below the bluff. A berm and wooden planks provided targets. The black powder groups greatly enjoyed the event, despite the usually freezing weather.

As the black powder and buckskinner activities grew in popularity, Steve Kemper began to invite the participants up from their frigid camp below the bluff to overnight in the new barracks rooms. In this photograph, sitting from left to right, Kemper shares a first meal in the barracks with Bill Ihm, Dave Romans, John Slader, Andy Russell, and Dick Hedges.

Some buckskinners began seeking a more specific persona to interpret. Rod Olsen and Dean Slader first restored an antique bellows that had been donated to the park before building what Slader laughingly dubbed a "semi-portable forge." The two began outdoor blacksmithing demonstrations in a grove south of the fort on summer weekends. The old bellows is still in use in the blacksmith shop.

By late 1980, the foundations were being laid for the second barracks. The completed archaeology visible here would be safe and sheltered beneath the new fort's floors. The excavated cellars seen in the center would be refilled and covered. New fireplaces would rise above the old bases revealed by the dig, like this one at the north (foreground) end of the line.

The ongoing plan to rebuild the fort now paralleled the developing efforts to repopulate the site with interpreters. By the summer of 1981, the foundation was laid for the north end of the west wall. With that accomplished, work began on building the rest of the entire barracks line. The brick walk and visitor center trailer are visible to the right.

With a new shipment of lumber from a small logging firm in New Mexico, the log walls of the second barracks building began rising. Utilizing the expertise they had gained in erecting the first barracks, Steve Kemper and his small parks crew were now able to work more speedily and with greater skill to finish the timbers and put this large and complex construction together.

As the barracks walls rose, masons began work on constructing the large and solid brick fireplaces and chimneys that would warm the rooms. This 1982 photograph shows one room with a finished fireplace and limestone hearth with a plank floor in place, awaiting only the chinking of the gaps in its logs to be complete.

Here the entire line of the new barracks can be seen in its nearly finished state. All chimneys are in place, the roofs are sheathed and shingled, door and window frames are installed, and the plank boardwalk is complete. With the final stage of filling the gaps with chinking and wattle, the structure would be ready for use by 1984.

With the success of the blacksmith demonstrations and a surplus of wood from the barracks construction, Steve Kemper approached Rod Olsen and Dean Slader in 1983 with an idea. Since the footprint of the original armorers' shop was well identified, would the two be willing to take on its reconstruction? The ready answer of Olsen and Slader was, "Well, why not?"

Slader and Olsen would be taking on a three-year labor of love to raise the structure. Shaping the logs would itself consume one year. With the walls beginning to rise, the two men began work on the brick fireplace that would warm a gunsmith's room and the forge (seen here) for the adjoining blacksmith shop where they would heat their iron for shaping.

The fort site was humming with activity in 1985 with multiple projects underway. This aerial photograph shows a large-scale archaeological dig in progress on the north and east walls (at left and top). In the meantime, outlines have been marked out for the reconstruction of the entire south wall (at right). Beyond the south wall line can be seen piles of new logs just arriving for the construction.

Local newspapers extensively covered the activities that summer. This *Fort Calhoun Chronicle* photograph (looking eastward) shows the dig, headed by NSHS archaeologist Gayle Carlson, well underway on the north wall. Again, the raised cubes of earth mark the corners of the 5-foot squares that are individually excavated for features and artifacts. The rising walls of the armorers' shop can be seen in the background.

Meanwhile, lumber was arriving for the construction of the fort's walls. Burlington Northern Railroad, through its subsidiary Plum Creek Timber Company, had donated the wood. It would total some 6,000 logs and 200,000 board feet of rough-sawn lumber—30 flatcars worth. This was enough to rebuild the remaining three barracks lines and outbuildings as well.

In addition to the armory and the south wall, an even more momentous structure was rising at the site. Thanks to the efforts of Nebraska Game and Parks director Eugene Mahoney, *Omaha World-Herald* chairman Harold Andersen, and the Game and Parks Foundation, Omaha-based building firm Peter Kewitt and Sons and Burlington Northern Railroad each donated $150,000 to erect a permanent visitors center. (*Fort Calhoun Chronicle*.)

By the spring of 1986, the new visitors center was ready for its dedication. It was to be named for Harold Andersen in tribute to his accomplishments in preserving Nebraska's historical sites. The building was a sophisticated and state-of-the-art structure, with two exhibit galleries, a welcoming lobby, a theater showing a film of the fort's history, animated displays, and sculpted brick murals.

Jack Curran, a Lincoln, Nebraska, sculptor and wood carver, created murals in brick depicting period scenes and personalities including daily fort life, Jim Bridger, Omaha chief Big Elk, and the Lewis and Clark Expedition. Most adorn the walls of the interior, but this one is located outside, beside the main door, to welcome visitors. It depicts Col. Henry Atkinson and soldiers greeting representatives of the local tribes.

A major visitors center display is a large, detailed model of the fort as it originally looked. This angle is toward the north, with the armory visible just outside the upper-right corner. There are a number of other outbuildings, including the large residence below the bluff to the right. Visitors can compare this with the reconstructed fort of today.

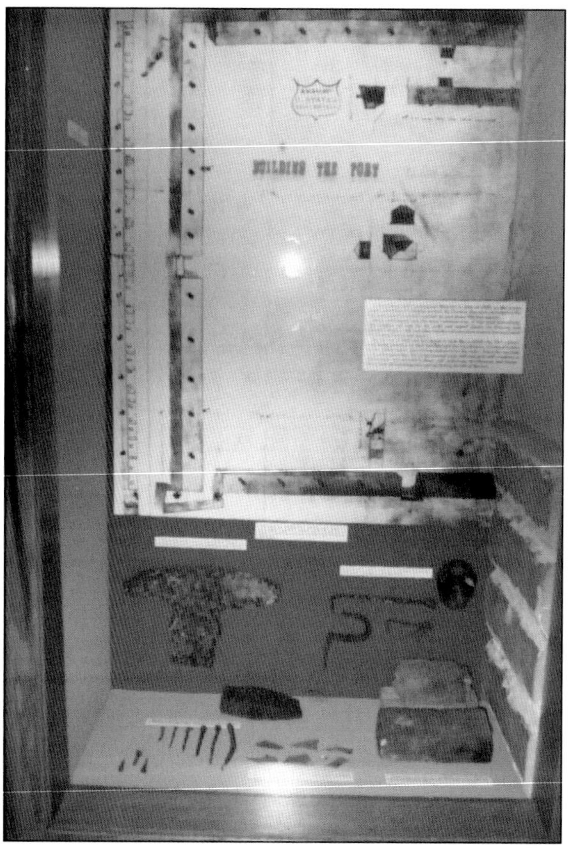

Many other exhibits in the two museum gallery spaces illustrate the fort's history and display a variety of some of the many period artifacts discovered at the site. The earlier Lewis and Clark visit is also depicted. Shown here is a display on the building of the original post. Visible are Talcott's plan, the axe head, bricks, nails, and other construction-related artifacts.

The May 18, 1986, dedication of the visitors center was a gala day for the park. A modern balloon ascension and a fly-over of the Strategic Air Command *Looking Glass* plane intermingled with period muzzle-loading and blacksmithing demonstrations. The ceremony, which also included the seasonal reopening of the park, drew over a thousand visitors.

This aerial shot provides a panorama of the whole park and shows the progress that year. In the foreground sits the new visitors center and its parking lot. In the upper left lies the angle of the rising fort with half of the south wall already erected. Curving in from the right, the park road connects the entrance, visitors center, and fort parking lot.

The visitors center dedication was a particularly proud and well-deserved moment for the dedicated staff who had worked so long to develop the state historical park and make it a success. Here, from left to right, assistant superintendent John Slader, superintendent Steve Kemper, his wife Jeanine, and visitor center receptionist Mary Fitzgerald pose before the Atkinson mural.

After opening ceremonies were performed by the SAC color guard (shown here), a number of dignitaries spoke to the assemblage. Michael Yanney, director of Nebraska Game and Parks, praised those of the public who had helped them raise the money, and James Hanson, historical society director, said Nebraskans should feel very proud of what they had accomplished.

Many dignitaries came from across the state to attend and take part in the visitors center's dedication ceremonies. Beyond the directors of the historical society and parks commission, they included state representatives, Omaha's mayor, and Harold Andersen (pictured at podium), for whom the new building was named. He gave the dedication address, thanking Eugene Mahoney (seated to the left of him) for his efforts in restoring the fort.

Other notables at the ceremony were Henry Atkinson's great-granddaughter Phyllis Atkinson Kennedy, Wade Miller of the Omaha tribal council, and Col. L. T. Wright of the 6th Infantry. Nebraska governor Bob Kerry also spoke (pictured here), promising the crowd that the park and restored fort would be enjoyed "for generations to come."

Work on the armorers' shop also concluded by the summer of 1986. A third volunteer, Wallace Merriam, joined Dean Slader and Rod Olsen in completing the log walls and building the roof. Here, from left to right, John Slader is aiding Dean and Wally in sheathing the rafters. The large doorway to the right is to the blacksmith's room, while the smaller one is to the gunsmith's.

The armory building had its own debut, welcoming visitors for the first time on the same day as the visitors center dedication and the seasonal opening for the park. It was considered one of the most finished features at the fort. The one-and-a-half story structure (see loft window to the left) has upper quarters, as it is believed the original craftsmen lived above their workshops.

The eastern room of the armory was occupied by the blacksmiths. Dean Slader and fellow volunteers (Tim Cuka seen here in the foreground) began their weekend demonstrations using the new forge to actually fashion ironwork for the fort. The forge and the two posts holding an anvil and a vise are placed exactly where archaeology showed the originals were.

The western room of the armory became a workshop for fort craftsmen. Here gunsmith Rich Flowers (left) and tinsmith (originally called a "whitesmith") Chris Hagemann pause in plying their meticulously learned antique skills. A fort-era musket hangs on the wall to the upper right. The original gunsmiths were responsible for maintaining or repairing the hundreds of weapons used by the garrison.

With barracks interior spaces now completed, volunteers began to move into the rooms and outfit them for specific new scenarios. One of the first additions was a cooper's workshop. A cooper is a maker of the buckets and barrels, which were vital necessities at the old fort. Seeking his own interpretive persona, Wallace Merriam taught himself the ancient and now almost extinct craft. (Mark Kennally.)

The role of carpenter was also added to the growing cast of fort players. This was another craft important to the old fort and just as important at the re-created one. Most of the fort's basic furnishings were and still are constructed in the carpentry shop. Volunteer Steve McAllister (seen here) set up the first shop in a barracks room near the west gate. Glen Story later took over the persona. (Blair *Pilot-Tribune*.)

A major addition to the fort's growing population was the Discovery Corps. This group specifically interpreted the Lewis and Clark Expedition on the Nebraska stretch of the Missouri River. Pictured here from left to right are (first row) Chris Vawter, Dwight Peters, Bob Dunn, Scott Moore, Tom Wood, and Jack Schmidt; (second row) Mike Vawter, Jim Drury, Dan Watson, Scott Davis, Glen Story, John Mitchell, Wade Davis, Wally Merriam, and Rich Flowers. (Rich Flowers.)

The Discovery Corps began making annual visits to the fort, setting up an encampment north of the quadrangle near the bluff edge. Seeking yet more unique and challenging personas, several of the members would begin interpreting the period of the fort, forming the foundation of what would become the official living history program. (Rich Flowers.)

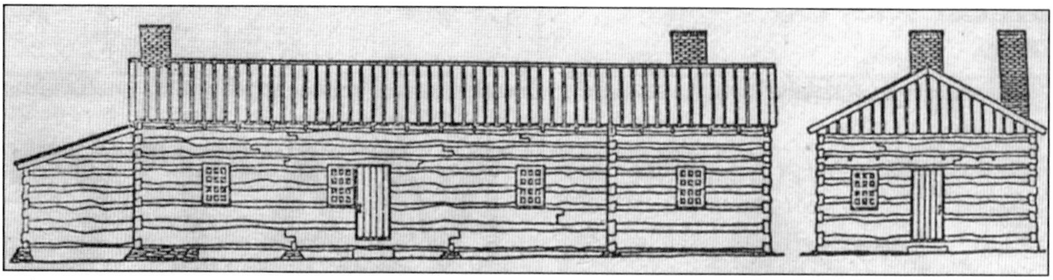

What Eugene Mahoney called "a key part of the entire Fort Atkinson project" was begun in 1986. This was a replica of the Council House, the scene of Indian–federal government treaty signings in the 1820s. It was to be erected on the original site, established by NSHS archaeological digs and a magnetometer survey by University of Nebraska physics professor John Weymouth. This drawing shows the proposed structure. (Nebraska State Game and Parks.)

The dig and survey identified the general size and configuration of the building and the locations of two fireplaces. It also identified that Indian artifacts were present. Again, the park's crew did the construction work, at which they had become quite proficient by now. Jerry Farber, the parks commission carpenter, works at shingling the two-story roof.

Superintendent Steve Kemper himself, by necessity a jack-of-all-trades, worked to design and then build the fireplaces with Jerry Farber's assistance. There were two fireplaces: a massive one for the main meeting hall, and a smaller one for a separate living quarters in the building. They utilized the popular 18th-century Count Rumford design for a better draft.

The Council House was completed in 1987. It is seen here with the Discovery Corps encampment set up nearby. The building had a main council room of 20 feet by 56 feet, which was entered by doors on either side. South of it, through the doorway to the left, was a smaller 14-foot-by-20-foot section that was perhaps the Indian agent's quarters.

Parleys with Indian tribes as well as fort group activities like banquets, dances, and plays were held in the main hall of the Council House. Chris Edmunds, as an Indian agent's wife, sits before the large fireplace. The main door to the right leads outside. All wood furnishings, the iron door hardware, and the chandeliers were produced by the fort carpenters and blacksmiths.

It was in the large council room that numerous significant treaties were concluded, including the only international treaty signed in Nebraska. South of the main room, through a separating doorway, were the Indian agent's quarters. Here, Indian agent Doug Kuony (left) and visiting trapper Wade Davis relax and enjoy playing some period music in a Fort Atkinson postcard.

In 1988, the first regular interpretive weekends were scheduled. They included a new group, formed by some of the Discovery Corps members, representing a unit of the fort's 1st Rifle Regiment. From left to right, Steve Grant, Mike Heil, Gary Hoover, Kevin Longeran, and John Kalish form up before the new south barracks to parade on the Independence Day weekend. The unit flag and the uniforms were all created by the group.

The fort garrison was also responsible for firing the cannon, which was always a crowd pleaser. The single fort artillery piece at this point was still "Little Richard," now reseated in a new, garrison-style gun carriage. Mike Heil loads the piece for a salute, while Gary Hoover (left), Bill Hartzell (center), and John Kalish watch, and a crowd (in background) keeps a safe distance.

By the end of the decade, Fort Atkinson had all the separate and distinctive interpretive units that form the living history program. These included the now-divided Discovery Corps and Rifles groups shown here, trapper/traders and other civilians, and tradesmen like the blacksmiths and cooper.

The first female interpreters were added to the fort at this time. Chris Eller (left) and Donella Patalon are clearing away lunch dishes in preparation for resuming candle making (in front). Chris, a talented spinner, would also begin the spinners and weavers scenario, one of the largest and most popular. (Blair *Enterprise*.)

Extra crowd-pleasing treats were added to the repertoire for the big Heritage Day weekends in October. Bill Drefs, portraying the fort butcher, slaughtered a hog, explaining what cuts he was making and how techniques differed in the fort era. Volunteer Gordie Whitcom dished out cooked sausage samples from a cast-iron kettle in the gunsmith's shop. (Blair *Enterprise*.)

With a growing presence of both soldier and trapper/trader interpreters, it was determined that a site separate from the fort's military scenarios was needed. Discovery Corps members set about building a trappers' cabin north of the fort in the late 1980s. They began by laying the sill logs just east of their camp on the bluff edge.

The 1980s ended with a visit by another Nebraska political personage. Gov. Kay Orr was taken on a tour of the park, beginning with the visitors center. To the left of her in the lobby is a case with period Indian and Rifleman mannequins. On the wall behind Steve Kemper are large versions of peace medallions carried by Lewis and Clark. Kemper would soon be leaving after 20 years as superintendent.

Governor Orr also toured the fort and examined the new construction. She was treated to a demonstration of log hewing by assistant superintendent John Slader, who would soon assume the position of park superintendent. Her visit to observe all the new developments at Fort Atkinson SHP was symbolic of how far the park had come over the past 20 years.

Six

Building the Living History

A new decade saw more dramatic changes at the fort. The living history program continued to expand, creating a formal Friends of Fort Atkinson (FoFA) organization by 1995. It established bylaws, gathered research, and began work on finding or crafting the necessary clothing, equipment, and paraphernalia needed to accurately re-create this unique period. A third, northern wall of the barracks quadrangle went up in the early 1990s. With many principal structures of the fort complete, work now focused on developing interpretive spaces for public view. Barracks rooms were fitted out as an engineer's office, with displays of the fort's construction and a typical officer's quarters. The cabin, originally planned as a trapper's residence, was now furnished as a sutler's store. By the mid-1990s, displays were also created for guardhouse and punishment rooms and for a fort hospital (the first in Nebraska). These, like the engineer's and officer's rooms, would be open to visitors whenever the park was open. Other spaces, like the armory and sutler's store, would be opened and populated on living history days.

To these and the already established interpretive rooms, the growing cadre of interpreters began eagerly adding new scenarios. Barracks rooms were set up for the soldiers, each with a connecting room for the company's kitchen and mess. To equip and uniform the military units, a quartermaster room was established. For those in command, an officer's kitchen and mess room were created. FoFA members seeking their own, separate personas set up spaces for the fort laundresses and created quarters for married and for bachelor officers. The fort surgeon received his own quarters, the commanding officer a day office, and the garrison school (another Nebraska first) was re-created. A bakery with a period oven was also constructed.

The later 1990s saw bigger structural additions to the fort site. Covered porches were added to the boardwalks. Most significantly, the stone-walled powder magazine, once the fort's most substantial feature, was rebuilt in the center of the parade ground.

By the turn of the millennium, Fort Atkinson was truly hitting its stride, ready to sprint into the next century.

In 1990, the responsibilities of park superintendent passed from Steve Kemper, who had so ably shepherded the site's development for 20 years, into the equally capable hands of John Slader (left). In turn, his previous position as assistant superintendent fell to Jerry Farber. The two would be responsible for further development of the fort itself and of a viable living history program.

The development of the fort continued with more work on rebuilding the walls of the barracks quadrangle. The west end of the north wall (seen here) was complete by the end of 1990, and the east half of the north wall was finished in 1992. This once again enclosed the parade ground of the original fort on the bluff.

When Mary Lou Dobson (right) and friend Emily Snide (far left), accomplished spinners and weavers, joined the living history group, that growing scenario was moved to an adjoining pair of rooms in the south barracks. Over the following years, many interpreters have entertained the public with these fascinating crafts, including Jacqueline Ericson (second from left) and Patty Wilson.

Bob Dobson, husband of spinner/weaver Marylou, took on the persona of army engineer Lieutenant Talcott when an engineer's room was created in the fort. It contained an exhibit on how the fort was reconstructed. Dobson showed visitors Talcott's plan and explained the methods used to design and build the original fort.

In 1992, it was also decided that the cabin beyond the Council House be fitted out as a sutler's store. Jerry Farber finished the interior with a fireplace, shelves for merchandise, and a counter for the proprietor. Over the years it became the site for various scenarios. When the sutler later moved into a new building, it reverted to its original purpose as a residence for a trapper.

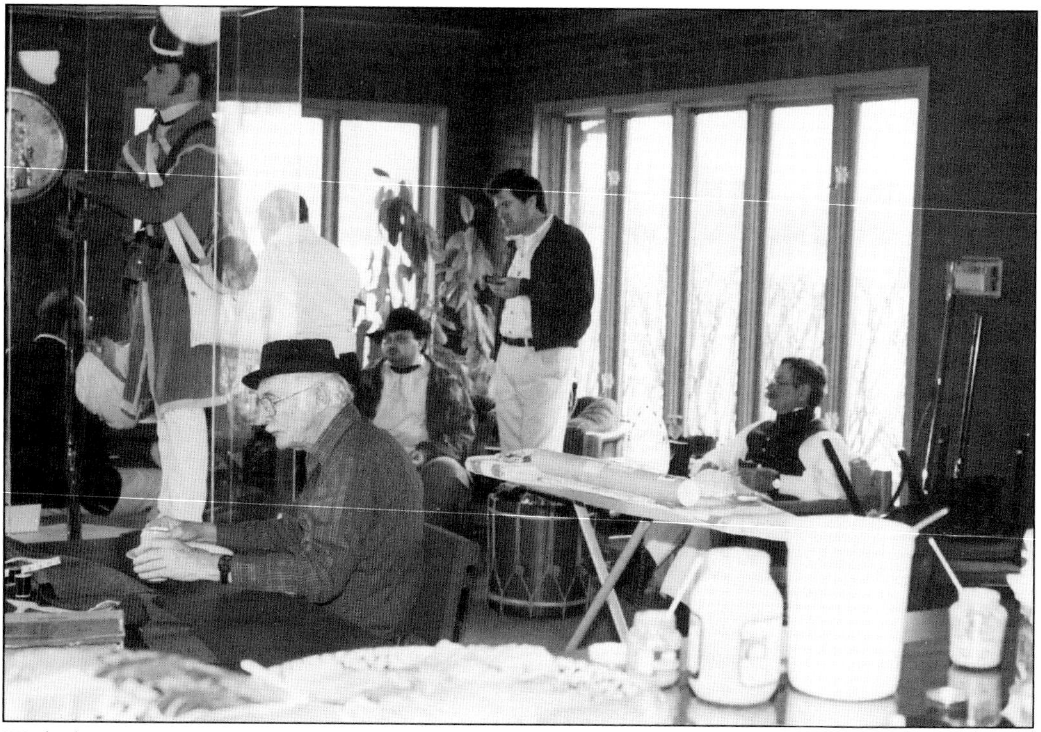

With the growing company of living history folks now interested in forming a stronger program, a symposium was organized in the spring of 1993. It was the beginning of an annual April workshop for the group. People met at the visitors center and learned to create historically accurate clothing and uniforms. This was critical because period equipment and dress were rare; it necessitated hand-making almost everything.

War of 1812 military expert Steve Abolt (at the sewing machine) led the hands-on demonstrations. The volunteers learned pattern construction and the cutting and sewing of pants, forage caps, coats, and anything else needed. Most vitally, this included uniform parts for both infantry and rifle regiments. After the demonstrations, they fell to on their portable sewing machines to practice.

Finished barracks rooms were turned into display areas that visitors could view any day the park was open. One of the first was a punishment room fitted with period instruments used to discipline soldiers. They included the stocks, a wooden horse, a punishment box, and neck signs identifying crimes. Jacob McCarthy is demonstrating use of the leg stocks. The door to the right rear leads to the jail room.

In the room adjoining the punishment room, a fort jail exhibit was created. Here, in the old fort's time, soldiers were incarcerated in these cramped, wooden cells. In this photograph, infantrymen Kris Ericson and Gavin Flint, seen through the exhibit's protective glass, stand guard on a deserting soldier awaiting his court-martial.

The growth of the military units, the old fort's most important population, brought a number of additional interpretive spaces to be developed for the soldiers. Infantry and Rifles were provided barrack's sleeping quarters for enlisted men. Bob Mead (left) and Steve Baker stand in a typical rifle company barracks. Eight bunks in each room provided accommodations for half a company, with two men sharing a bed, sleeping head to toe.

Each sleeping quarters was connected to a second room. This was used as the company mess—a combined kitchen with fireplace and dining area with tables. Group activities, such as cleaning weapons and uniforms, also occurred there. Pictured here, from left to right, 6th Infantrymen Gavin Flint, John Schmidt, Michael Grierson, Kris Ericson, and Shane Johnson enjoy a midday meal.

Besides the corps of laundresses, the only females present at the old fort were the wives and daughters of the married officers. Quarters for officers with families were provided within the fort. Wealthier officers also built separate dwellings outside the quadrangle. Earley Smith, as Captain of Rifles, works at his desk in his quarters, furnished as that of a typical married officer.

For unmarried, lower-ranking officers like lieutenants, a Bachelors' Officers Quarters (BOQ) was provided. Junior officers shared the rooms, and officers gathered in the evenings for drink, talk, and cards. The rumored antics that these unattached and often young men got into caused such quarters to be nicknamed "Bedlam."

When Jack Schmidt and Earley Smith took on personas as fort officers, the two began development of other interpretive spaces that would have been available to those in command. As the officers would have had a separate and formal dining area, a kitchen and mess room were established. In the kitchen, Casey Ankenbauer (left) and Molly Lundgren prepare a meal to serve to the officers at midday.

The officer's mess was set up next door to the kitchen. Smith (second from left) and Schmidt (second from right) researched its proper period decor and supplied much of the furniture and accouterments themselves. Even in a far-frontier post, officers provided themselves with elegant and civilized surroundings. At the meal's conclusion, the two raise a toast with Bob Dobson (left) and Dan Watson.

To help provide some necessary sustenance to the soldiers' mess and demonstrate more early techniques to the visitors, a buttery room was also established. The methods of churning and producing the butter during the old fort's period were utilized. Here officers' cook Julie Ashton (right) procures fresh butter from Arlis Ded to prepare the day's meal.

The officer in charge of the fort's daily activities worked from a commander's day office. This was established in a room by the main, western gate. It also served as a storehouse for official papers, equipment, the American flag, and the flags of both regiments. Tom Wood, in the persona of commanding officer, explains the orders of the day to his adjutant, Bob Baker.

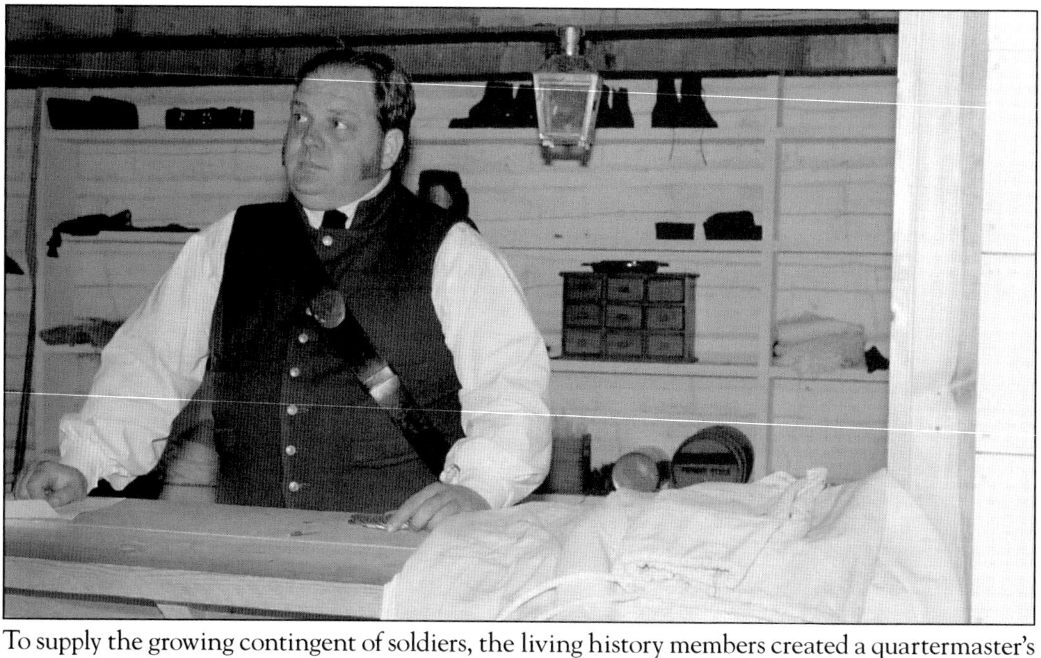

To supply the growing contingent of soldiers, the living history members created a quartermaster's store. This interpretive area would both be functional and have an exhibit aspect. On any day, the room's contents could be viewed through a window. On living history weekends it could be opened to supply uniforms and equipment to the garrison. John Oien, a fort musician, also functioned as the first quartermaster.

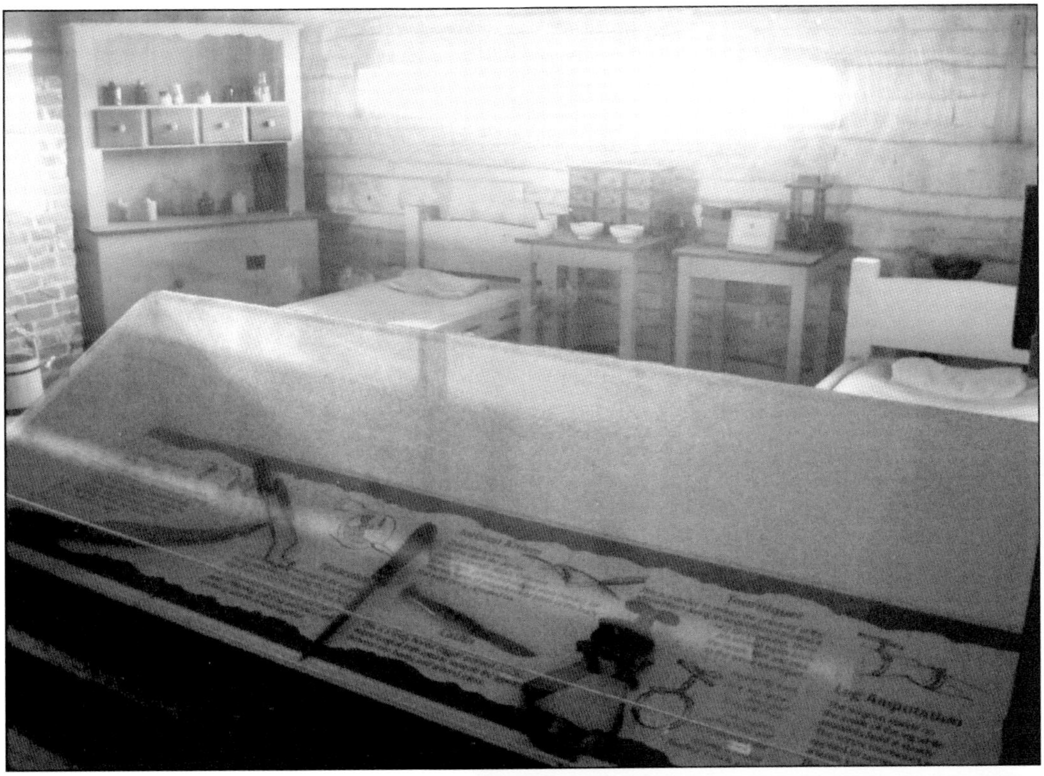

One of the most interesting exhibits created was of the fort's hospital, the first one in Nebraska. Here are the beds and other furnishings, as well as a display of some of the instruments used by the 1820s surgeons. Many of these devices of crude, early medicine seem quite diabolical today, as they were used mostly to bleed, leech, and purge body fluids or to cut off damaged limbs.

As part of his college history program, Wade Davis did the research to accurately outfit a surgeon's office next to the hospital. He was also first to portray the surgeon, doing medical scenarios such as an amputation. Assistant surgeon Mark Kennally demonstrates pulling a tooth (without painkillers) from soldier Kyle Ankenbauer. The top of the surgeon's operating table was painted black to disguise any stains from blood.

With the cabin completed, Bill Grierson (seen with his wife, Jan) moved into it in 1993, assuming the persona of James Kennerly, the old fort's sutler. The sutler's job was to supply merchandise to the garrison, much as a post exchange (PX) does today. By the following season, Grierson would be both interpreting the historical scenario of serving the soldiers and selling real period goods to the modern public.

After Grierson began interpreting the sutler, his wife expressed an interest in creating her own persona near the cabin. Jerry Farber cheerfully accommodated her by creating a period bake oven site between the cabin and the Council House. Dave Maron (seen here) later took over the role as "Baker Dude" for the group, preparing and baking fresh bread every living history weekend.

Laundresses were an integral part of the old fort's garrison. Part of an official unit of the army, each one did the laundry for half a company. Terese Peters was the first to interpret the scenario. Here Emily Snide (left) and Carolyn Larsen work outside the north gate. Emily is washing clothing with a wooden maul, while Carolyn mends a soldier's tunic. The triangular object in the center is a lye leacher for making soap.

Another of the many fort firsts was the first school in Nebraska. It was re-created so both fort children and young visitors could experience the educational methods of the 1820s, studying period textbooks and writing lessons on slates. At the old fort, a soldier took on the teacher's role; he was paid with a liquor allotment of two gallons per month. In this picture, Erin Davis (center) plays the teacher.

In 1995, the living history volunteers officially chartered a Friends of Fort Atkinson organization. Their first major event was a "Muster up the Missouri" involving 100 volunteers from nine states. Saluting the raising of the colors are, from left to right, Bob Dorian as surgeon, Earley Smith as lieutenant, soldiers John Fenner, Jay Kelgor, Dustin Jeck, and Dean Dingman, fifer Bob Dunn, Dan Watson as brevet major, and drummer Scott Moore.

During the always-ongoing research into the fort's past, Jerry Farber came across an enlightening court-martial record. A soldier was tried for leaving his post in the rain to stand under a porch. This corroborated a belief that the old fort's boardwalks had been covered. In 1997, the Nebraska Game and Parks staff went to work adding the porches.

A major addition was made to the fort artillery in 1997. With foundation funding, a 6-pounder cannon tube, like one of the period, was purchased. Earley Smith and Chris Hagemann fetched the barrel from its East Coast manufacturer. It was first mounted on a garrison carriage built at the fort. Hagemann named the gun Gustav (nicknamed "Gus") after his grandfather.

The year of 1997 also saw a new archaeological dig on the powder magazine location in preparation for reconstruction. The original structure was the fort's most substantial feature: 16 feet by 26 feet with stone walls 2 feet thick. It had survived destruction of the rest of the fort by over 30 years. Workmen from Nebraska Game and Parks accurately re-created its heavy stone walls from records, the old plans, and the dig information.

The powder magazine, which was a storehouse for the considerable amount of black powder needed at the fort, was placed in the center of the parade ground. It was also the only building constructed of stone. Both of these features were intended to minimize damage to the fort should the powder blow up. An explosion, contained by the walls, would shoot upward, safely away from the distant barracks.

Shelves within the building were stocked with powder cartridges for rifles and muskets, artillery loads, and even period hand grenades. The structure was completed and dedicated in 1998. Funding to resurrect this key fort structure was provided by a grant from Heather Davis, her parents William E. and Rose Marie, and their Davis Foundation.

Seven

Developing for the Future

With the new century, Fort Atkinson and its living history program continued to expand. New interpretive spaces were added. A particularly major one was a new Sutler's Store, built specifically for the purpose. More barracks rooms were set up. One represented living quarters for a laundress married to a soldier, while another housed a fort library (another Nebraska first) with some 600 period books plus newspapers. A quilting room was also established. A non-period archaeology room was created where children could dig up artifacts. Outside the quadrangle, a fort garden was cultivated to represent the post's huge agricultural output.

The role of the military expanded. The living history weekends came to include the whole daily routine of period military life. Reveille, roll call, regular duties, drill, meals, and retreat were all included. In addition, scenarios were incorporated into the day showing the public how such things as the courts-martial and pay calls were conducted. Special, larger scenarios were developed for holiday weekends like Memorial Day and the Fourth of July.

As Fort Atkinson began to close with its 200th anniversary, one major focus became the maintenance of what had already been created. With major budgetary concerns, the foundation and FoFA redoubled its efforts to increase public awareness of the site and raise the funds needed to insure that this special place not disappear beneath the sod again.

This did not mean that further improvements would not continue into the future. For the living history program, this meant increasing efforts to recruit more members, enlarging the program, creating yet more scenarios, and gaining greater publicity. For the fort site, there would be continued planning for more structures, including archaeology displays, a commander's house, and other outbuildings such as a school and a band room.

As of 2010, plans were underway to erect a period-correct flagpole. A memorial dedicated to the hundreds of fort dead was also being developed. This would include the civilian men, women, and children who inhabited the bluff. But it would especially be a place for remembrance of the many soldiers, both enlisted men and officers, who gave their lives for their country in a place very far from home.

In 2000, construction of another major feature for the fort commenced. This was a new, separate, and larger Sutler's Store, this time built expressly for the purpose. It can be seen underway to the right, above the armorers' shop. This aerial photograph demonstrates the enormous progress at fort rebuilding that had been accomplished over the past 20 years, especially when comparing this shot with that on the prospectus cover (page 41).

The Sutler's Store opened in 2000. For the first time, the fort had a structure comparable to what would have served the original garrison. The large main section behind the sign contained the merchandise. The smaller section to the right was the sutler's living quarters. Like the powder magazine, this store was made possible by a grant from Heather Davis and the William E. and Rose Marie Davis Foundation.

Sutler Bill Grierson (right), seen here with his assistant Stephen Juza, was instrumental in designing and equipping the interior of the store. All the merchandize is either interpretive material supplied by funding from the Fort Atkinson Foundation or real, period-correct products—many made by fort craftsmen—that can be purchased by visitors. On living history days, the store is one of the most popular spots at the fort. (Teena Rawlings.)

A new addition to the many interpretive locations was a room depicting the quarters for common soldiers married to laundresses. These rooms were shared with another couple, each pair sleeping in a single bunk. Children slept on pallets on the floor. Here Judy Flint helps mend a bonnet for her daughter-in-law Melissa. (Teena Rawlings.)

The fort library, another Nebraska first, was also added to the list of interpretive rooms. Contrary to popular belief, there were many literate soldiers in the garrison. Seeking to foster this, Colonel Leavenworth created the library, which had 600 volumes and subscribed to 23 newspapers. Books were checked out and fines were collected just as they are today. Gavin Flint interprets as fort librarian.

A garden was also created between the north gate and the Council House. It was planted with period-correct vegetables and herbs. This would represent both the individual company gardens that supplied the soldier's kitchens and the huge amount of agricultural activity that took place at the old fort. Then soldiers tended the crops, devoting much of their fatigue duty to farming. Today Kris and Kristy Ericson are the gardeners.

The ladies of the old fort practiced many crafts popular in the day. One of those most interesting to visitors is quilting. A craft room was set up so those women portraying the wives and daughters of fort officers could practice and interpret the sewing skills needed. Danion Mead (right) and Penny Ankenbauer work at the quilt frame while Connie Wheeler embroiders.

One of the most recent sites created was an archaeology room. It was set up in a dirt-floored barracks room so younger visitors could experience what the original digs were like. Each child can excavate a square of ground to discover replica artifacts like those actually recovered. Judy Flint points out what type of artifact this girl has found. Diggers occasionally find real artifacts in the old fort's soil.

During the summer of 2004, Fort Atkinson received a third cannon, the second of the big 6-pounders to be financed by the foundation. This one was dubbed Wally in honor of old-guarder Wallace Merriam (behind cannon). Like predecessor Gus, it was a purchased tube with a carriage built by the fort carpenters and blacksmiths. The soldiers gathered at the Armory for its test firing.

Fort Atkinson living history days now involved scenarios re-creating every aspect of the old fort garrison's day. Each day began with reveille, a first assembly of soldiers, and a raising of the flag with a cannon salute. Here the Infantry, Rifle, and Artillery units are drawn up with drummer Curt Isaacson (left). (Teena Rawlings.)

These members of the 6th Infantry—from left to right, Gavin Flint, Mike Grierson, Bill Jordan, and Kris Ericson—prepare for a demonstration in marching and firing. Most of the elaborate clothing and equipment seen here must be painstakingly made from scratch. All the volunteer soldiers at Fort Atkinson have gone to great efforts to arm, uniform, and train themselves for an accurate depiction of the period garrison.

The soldiers' routines for the interpretive weekend follow those of an 1820 soldier's typical day. It was spent on drills in marching and fighting, cleaning weapons and uniforms, housekeeping and maintenance chores, and leisure-time activities. These members of the Artillery, Rifles, and Infantry are performing a practice skirmish—advancing, retreating, and firing volleys. (Teena Rawlings.)

Additional scenarios depicting other aspects of the old fort's life were developed and incorporated into interpretive weekends. In that early period of much crueler punishments, a soldier who had violated regulations—in this case by desertion—was marched around the parade ground by guards, led with an iron neck collar. Some offenders were forced to wear signs proclaiming their crimes.

Serious crimes were dealt with by a court-martial. The case was judged by three field-grade officers (major and above). Here the court is set up outside as a "drumhead" court-martial because, on the battlefield, a drum was often literally used as the judges' bench. Popular trial scenarios include desertion, murder, laundresses selling liquor, drunkenness, and mutiny.

Paydays at the far-frontier fort were months apart. When the paymaster visited, pay call became a major event for the soldiers eager for their meager earnings. Acting paymaster Bill Grierson (right foreground) is doling out the proper amount to each soldier while officer Jack Schmidt (right background) observes. The head laundress, seated beyond Grierson, makes sure each soldier pays the amount he owes for laundry services. (Bob Ericson.)

An important daily ritual at old Fort Atkinson was the liquor ration. In the post–War of 1812 era, soldiers (and laundresses) still received a gill (4 ounces) of rum or whiskey per day. Here quartermaster Bob Baker passes out a ration to Eddie Wood, while following officer Tom Wood makes sure each soldier consumes all the "liquor" on the spot to prevent hoarding it for a drinking binge. (Devin Flint.)

Although most of the communication between Fort Atkinson and civilization far downriver was by boat, a more direct route from the Council Bluff to Chariton, Missouri, 350 miles away was marked out in 1820. When urgent orders or information had to be carried to the post, it was done by horse. Messenger Bill Jordan is seen delivering his mail to the post commander.

One of the most significant treaties negotiated at the fort was between the Mexican government and the chiefs of the Pawnee nation. As the only international treaty concluded in what would become Nebraska, it is yet another fort first. Fort commander Jack Schmidt greets Wade Davis (center) as the leader of the Mexican delegation, while Indian agent Doug Kuony (in white coat) acts as liaison.

A death at the fort was the occasion for a major and solemn ceremony. A funeral party was organized to move the deceased to a last resting place in the fort's cemetery where a burial service was held. Although scores of military and civilian souls perished during old Fort Atkinson's era, including over 160 during the scurvy epidemic, the exact place where they still lie has yet to be discovered. (Teena Rawlings.)

In contrast with the funeral, the most lighthearted event for Fort Atkinson occurs on the closing living history days during the first weekend of October. Many visitors come on these usually bright and brisk fall days. The volunteers come in especially large numbers for their last yearly chance to interpret. Special scenarios, like this pressing of apple cider by Chris Hagemann (center) and Kristy Ericson (right), delight the crowds. (Bob Ericson.)

As the living history program at Fort Atkinson SHP grew, other living history interpreters—individuals and groups—from similar period organizations all across the country began to visit the site. This red-coated Lewis and Clark fife and drum corps from Missouri marches with the garrison in a trooping of the regimental colors, led by officer James Lundgren.

In the early 2000s, a candlelight tour was added to the living history program on the first Saturday of November. This nighttime scenario offered a different view of the fort's life, allowing tours of visitors to peek in on the garrison's evening activities. Here, in the Sutler's Store, officers play cards while the Indian agent looks on. (Bob Ericson.)

The biggest living history event at Fort Atkinson comes on the weekend nearest the Fourth of July. The major activity is the garrison Independence Day celebration. This includes a grand parade of review by the troops, followed by a reading of the Declaration of Independence. After this the Rifles, Infantry, and Artillery perform a salute to the states, firing a volley as the name of each is read.

Other of the Independence Day's diverse entertainments include bake sales, children's games, and an ice-cream social. Here, in the locust grove west of the Council House, toasts to the president and the nation are offered by the officers, while fort musicians provide a concert for the crowd. The original grove was planted by Colonel Leavenworth for his wife.

The greatest crowd-pleasing event of Independence Day follows the salute to the states. Up comes a rolling barrage, with each cannon and unit of soldiers firing in turn. This culminates with everyone—Rifles, Infantry and the Artillery battery—firing a volley in unison. The combined explosion shakes the ground and fills the air with fire and smoke in a satisfying conclusion to a most fitting 4th of July experience. (Devin Flint.)

With the conclusion of each living history day comes the retreat. While the visitors watch, the garrison forms up at the drummer's call to march to the flagpole. A cannon fires a salute as the national colors are lowered. Thus do the interpreters of Fort Atkinson, this once-lost historical site now so lovingly restored, end their public hours. (Author's collection.)

An important new feature for 2011 is a memorial to all those brave and pioneering inhabitants who perished at Fort Atkinson. As this drawing indicates, it is an enclosed yard near the locust grove with a monument and a list of everyone interred in the as-yet unidentified cemetery. It is hoped that one day the rediscovered dead will be officially reinterred in consecrated ground atop the Council Bluff.

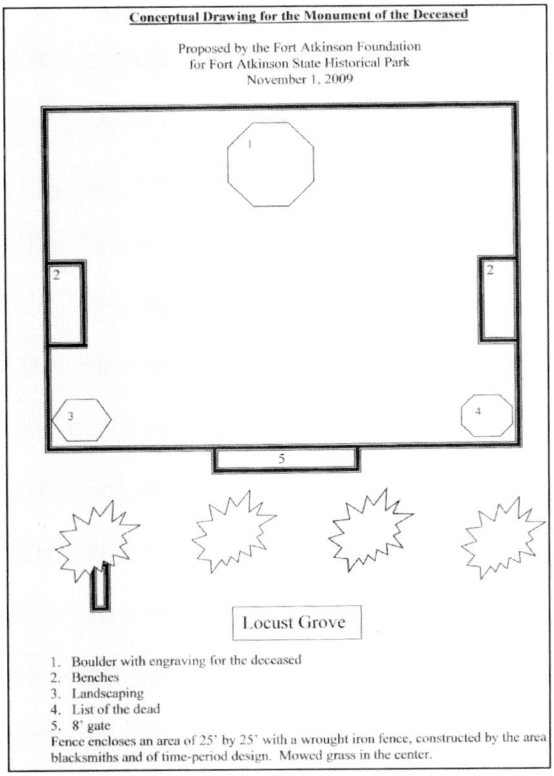

The final image of the old flagpole is a fitting conclusion to this book. Eighty-three years after its dedication, NSHS's Gayle Carlson (right) did a dig on the monument for John Slader (center) in preparation for replacing it with a period-correct flagpole. It would be moved to a new location in the parking lot, thus ending its long, loyal, and often lonely service in keeping Fort Atkinson's memory alive.